Governance
Handbook

For Trustees of
Academies,
Multi-academy Trusts
and Governors of
Maintained Schools

SCHOLASTIC

Scholastic Education, an imprint of Scholastic Ltd
Book End, Range Road, Witney, Oxfordshire, OX29 0YD
Registered office: Westfield Road, Southam, Warwickshire CV47 0RA

www.scholastic.co.uk

© 2016, Scholastic Ltd

123456789 6789012345

British Library Cataloguing-in-Publication Data
A catalogue record for this book is available from the British Library.

ISBN 978-1407-16077-1
Printed by Ashford Colour Press

Authors
Department for Education

Editorial
Rachel Morgan

Design
Neil Salt

Cover design
Neil Salt

Contents

Section 10 – Admissions and organisational changes 66

Section 11 – Control and community use of school premises 72

Section 12 – School finance 77

Section 13 – Information sharing 91

Section 14 – Support to be effective 97

SCHOLASTIC

Foreword

Governing boards are the strategic decision makers and vision setters in every school and academy. They play a vital role in ensuring the best possible education for every child by creating robust accountability for school leaders. Crucially, that means using and being familiar with objective data on the performance of pupils, teachers and finances to ask the right questions and ensure resources are allocated to school priorities. It also means ensuring that schools prepare pupils for life and the workplace by building their character and resilience and by implementing their Prevent duty to protect them from the risks of extremism and radicalisation.

As we move towards an increasingly school-led system, the importance of boards' role will only continue to grow. A school-led system doesn't mean schools working in isolation; it means schools that are fully integrated with their local community and, crucially, connected with and learning from each other. I want to see more schools seeking out opportunities to collaborate. I believe there are still many cases in which pupils would benefit from their school being part of something bigger. Governors, like parents and headteachers, can be passionate about their school. But pupils must come before adults. The academy sector is leading the way with 85% of all new academies in 2014/15, and overall, 57% of all open academies, part of a multi-academy trust in which a single board oversees all the academies in the trust.

Working together is about better teaching and a broader curriculum for pupils; greater leadership and development opportunities for teachers; and more efficiency and impact from financial and other resources. These benefits are most fully realised when school-to-school collaboration is consolidated through formalised cross-school governance arrangements. When boards govern a group of schools we also then see further improvement in the quality of governance – as boards gain a more strategic perspective. The principles of effective governance are well-established and increasingly understood. But governing a group of schools is different to governing a single school. An independent review of a board's effectiveness is needed to ensure it is ready for growth.

All boards, however many schools they govern, need people with skills appropriate to the scale and nature of their role; and no more people than they need to have all the necessary skills.

Many boards are already reaping the rewards of recruiting people from business. The reforms we have introduced make it easier for boards to recruit a wide mix of highly-skilled people and I call on more schools to make use of Academy Ambassadors, SGOSS Governors for Schools and the Education & Employers Taskforce who we are funding to help them do so.

This 'Governance handbook' has been re-named to make clear that it applies to all those involved in governance. It now refers throughout to the 'board' to emphasise that it applies equally to the governing body of a small maintained school as it does to the board of a large MAT. I want everyone involved in governance to be confident in tackling underperformance, challenging mediocrity, and setting the highest of expectations; refusing to accept second best for any child. I hope you find this handbook a valuable resource to support you in your role.

John Nash Parliamentary Under Secretary of State for Schools

About the 'Governance handbook'

Aim

The 'Governance handbook' is departmental advice from the Department for Education. It sets out the government's vision and priorities for effective school governance, and:

- outlines the core role and functions of the board of governors in maintained schools and academies ("the board");
- summarises and provides a first point of reference on all the legal duties on boards, signposting to more detailed information, guidance and resources; and
- provides information on the support available to boards to be effective.

Review date

The 'Governance handbook' is kept under review and updated to reflect changes to the law affecting boards of governors and changes to education policy – usually twice a year.

Who is this advice for?

This handbook is for:

- Governors, headteachers, clerks and others with an interest in the governance of maintained schools; and
- Members, trustees, local governors, principals, clerks and others with an interest in the governance of academy trusts and multi-academy trusts.

Unless otherwise stated, references to 'the board' should be taken to refer to the accountable body. In the case of maintained schools, this will be the governing body and in a single or multi-academy trust (MAT), it will be the board of trustees. Where the responsibilities of the board are discussed, this should be taken to refer to the responsibilities of the accountable body, or in a MAT to any local governing body (LGB) or other committee to which the board has delegated responsibility (but not accountability) for the governance function in question.

References to 'governors' means whomever is responsible for fulfilling governance functions – whether that be the governors of a maintained school, the trustees of an academy or MAT, or the local governors to whom the function in question has been delegated within a MAT. However, when specific reference is made to particular governance roles in an academy context the term 'trustee' will be used for those on the board of the trust and 'local governor' for those on a LGB. References to academies include free schools, university technical colleges (UTCs) and studio schools. The handbook does not apply directly to pupil referral units, sixth-form colleges and general further education colleges though they may find its general principles helpful.

Section 1 – The essentials of effective governance

1. All boards, whether in the maintained or academy sector and no matter how many schools they are responsible for, have three core functions:

   1. **Ensuring clarity of vision, ethos and strategic direction;**
   2. **Holding the headteacher to account for the educational performance of the school and its pupils, and the performance management of staff; and**
   3. **Overseeing the financial performance of the school and making sure its money is well spent.**

2. The core features of effective governance also apply at any scale and in any context, and are common to good governance practice in the charity and corporate sectors. They include the importance of the board having:

   - The right people with the necessary skills, time and commitment, and sufficient diversity of perspectives to ensure internal challenge, all actively contributing in line with clearly defined roles and responsibilities under an effective chair and an explicit code of conduct, and with active succession planning;

   - Clear governance structures with tightly defined remits, particularly in relation to functions delegated to committees or other bodies;

   - Clear separation between the strategic and operational in terms of the role of the board and its school leaders;

   - A positive relationship between the board and its school leaders enabling robust constructive challenge on the basis of a good understanding of objective data particularly on pupil progress, staff performance and finances;

   - The support and advice of an independent and professional clerk and, in the case of academies, company secretary;

   - Robust processes for financial and business planning and oversight and effective controls for compliance, propriety and value for money; and

   - Processes for regular self-evaluation, review and improvement including; skills audits, training and development plans, and independent external reviews as necessary.

3. Forming or joining a group of schools can help create more effective governance. The board that governs the group gains a more strategic perspective and the ability to create more robust accountability through the opportunity to compare and contrast between schools. The boards that decide to join a group are relieved of the burden of ultimate accountability and many welcome responsibility for financial and other corporate functions being carried centrally, leaving them freer to focus on pupil progress and attainment. Common governance also lays the foundation for a range of other benefits for pupils, staff and budgets, as discussed further in Section 3.

4. When a board decides to grow the number of schools it governs, it might try to develop its existing governance model to form a small MAT or federation of two or three schools, but growth beyond three schools usually represents the first real need to overhaul governance arrangements. Likewise, the governance structures of a small MAT will start to become stretched at around 6-7 schools and by 10 a further overhaul will be needed.

5. In order to transition to academy status or grow successfully from a single school into a small MAT or federation, and onward into a large MAT, the board should commission a robust independent review of its effectiveness and readiness for growth. The All Party Parliamentary Group for Governance and Leadership's Questions for boards and MAT boards to ask themselves provide a helpful framework for doing this. As the organisation the board is governing becomes larger and more complex organisationally and financially, governance can, and in some cases must, change in a number of ways:

   1. **Culture**: it is important to generate a professional ethos across the entire governance structure and a culture of one organisation and away from any sense of 'my school/ your school'.

   2. **Skills**: an increasing number of pupils and schools are impacted by the quality of the individuals on the board, and there is hence an increasing imperative for the board to act professionally and actively recruit, develop and retain high calibre board members and an effective chair with the necessary skills to govern and lead the increasingly complex organisation and oversee its growth.

   3. **Executive oversight**: there is increasing opportunity, and possibly need, for the board to discharge some of its functions of governance and oversight through a central professional executive team – starting with an executive principal and finance director, and with further growth extending to a chief executive officer.

   4. **Structures**: there is an expanding range of options for how to design governance structures and levels of delegation. As the need for additional tiers within non-executive and executive governance structures grows to avoid unwieldy spans of control, there is an increasing need for absolute clarity on the role and remit of each part of the structure and the relationship and reporting arrangements between them – including, for example in a MAT, between the role of a local governing body (LGB) and an executive principal in holding a school-level principal to account.

   5. **Processes**: there is an increasing need for the board to be professional in the way it conducts its business. It needs more standardised and robust systems and processes for governance and oversight, including systems for reporting and analysing school performance data; for financial planning, management and control; and for HR and other business processes. It also needs to ensure more standardised teaching and school improvement methodologies are in place across its schools based on proven pedagogies.

   6. **Risk**: increasingly, boards need a more sophisticated understanding of financial, organisational and educational risk; its assessment and its minimisation – and this in turn highlights that increasingly the board must be strategic, that it must focus on priorities and that it must manage by exception.

Section 2 – The core functions of the board

1. This section looks at the boards' three core functions of setting vision, holding the headteacher to account for the school's educational performance and ensuring money is well spent. The resources and support available to boards to help them deliver this role effectively are set out in Section 14.

2.1 Setting vision, ethos and strategic direction

2. Boards are the key strategic decision-making body of every school. It is their role to set the school's strategic framework and to ensure all statutory duties are met.

3. The board should ensure that the school has a clear vision – which it may be helpful to articulate in a specific written vision statement. This should include ambitions for current and future pupils, as well as for the school's relationship with other schools. For multi-academy trusts (MATs), the vision should set out the level of ambition they have for future growth.

4. The board should make sure there is a strategy in place for achieving this vision. The strategy should provide a robust framework for setting priorities, creating accountability and monitoring progress in realising the school's vision. The focus should be on significant strategic challenges. The detail of all the actions that will drive school improvement should be contained in a separate school improvement plan. Avoiding unnecessary detail and peripheral issues will prevent the board's attention being spread too thinly and help create a practical and powerful tool for facilitating its core business. The National Governors' Association (NGA) and the Wellcome Trust have jointly developed guidance to help boards develop a robust strategic Framework for Governance.

5. The board should set and safeguard a school ethos of high expectations of everyone in the school community. This includes high expectations for the behaviour, progress and attainment of all pupils and for the conduct and professionalism of both staff and governors.

6. Foundation governors, such as those appointed by a church or diocese, have a specific role in preserving and developing the ethos of the school, including any religious character. They must also ensure the school is conducted in accordance with the foundation's governing documents, including any trust deed relating to the school.

7. Every effort should be made to ensure the school's ethos promotes the fundamental British values of democracy, the rule of law, individual liberty, and mutual respect and tolerance for those with different faiths and beliefs; and encourage students to respect other people, with particular regard to the protected characteristics set out in the Equality Act 2010 and accompanying guidance. The board should ensure that this ethos is reflected and implemented effectively in school policy and practice and that there are effective risk assessments in place to safeguard and promote students' welfare. Departmental advice for maintained schools and academies on the spiritual, moral, social and cultural development of pupils includes references to promoting British values.

8. Boards are able to suspend any governor for acting in a way that is contrary to the ethos of the school. Swift action should be taken to suspend from office any governor that acts to undermine fundamental British values or the board's commitment or ability to deliver on its Prevent duty. The board, or where applicable other appointing body, should also consider removing from office any governor acting in this manner.

9. If you are concerned that a governor or potential governor may have links to extremism or that a child might be at risk of extremism, or if you have any other concern about extremism in a school please contact our helpline at counter.extremism@education.gsi.gov.uk or on 020 7340 7264.

2.2 Holding the headteacher to account

10. The second core function of all boards is holding the headteacher to account for the educational performance of the school and its pupils and the performance management of staff.

2.2.1 Boards' relationship with school leaders

11. Headteachers are responsible for the internal organisation, management and control of schools. It is their job to implement the strategic framework established by the board. Boards should work to support and strengthen the leadership of the headteacher or executive headteacher, and hold them to account for the day-to-day running of their school(s), including the performance management of staff. Boards should play a strategic role, and avoid routine involvement in operational matters. They should focus strongly on holding the headteacher to account for exercising their professional judgement in these matters and all of their other duties.

12. However, since the board is responsible in law for the school, it may need to intervene in operational matters if a circumstance arises where, because of the actions or inactions of the headteacher, the school may be in breach of a duty if the board did not intervene. Having advised the board, the headteacher must comply with any reasonable direction given by it.

13. One of the key characteristics expected of headteachers, as outlined within the National Standards of Excellence for Headteachers, is that they should welcome strong governance and actively support their board to understand its role and deliver its core functions effectively. Headteachers should therefore welcome and enable appropriately robust challenge by providing any data the board requests and responding positively to searching questions.

14. The relationship between the board and headteacher is discussed further in departmental advice on the Roles, Procedures and Allowances Regulations 2013. The NCTL report Headteacher Performance: Effective Management describes how boards can appraise and performance manage their headteacher effectively. The National Association of Headteachers (NAHT), the Association for College and School Leaders (ASCL) and the NGA has issued a joint statement on the principles for the working relationship between boards and school leaders. Further information on headteacher appraisal is available in Section 9.4.

15. The School teachers' pay and conditions document 2015 (STPCD) requires boards and headteachers to have regard to the need for the headteacher and teachers to be able to achieve a satisfactory balance between the time required to discharge their professional duties and the time required to pursue their personal interests outside work.

2.2.2 Asking the right questions

16. Effective boards hold their headteacher and other senior school leaders to account for improving pupil and staff performance by asking the right questions. It is essential that boards use and are familiar with specific data about their school to help inform these questions (see Sections 2.3 and 2.4 for more information). This might include asking:

- Which groups of pupils are the highest and lowest performing, and why? Do school leaders have credible plans for addressing underperformance or less than expected progress? How will we know that things are improving?

- How is the school going to raise standards for all children, including the most and least able, those with special educational needs, those receiving free school meals, boys and girls, those of a particular ethnicity, and any who are currently underachieving?

- Which year groups or subjects get the best and worst results and why? How does this relate to the quality of teaching across the school? What is the strategy for improving the areas of weakest performance?

- Is the school adequately engaged with the world of work and preparing their pupils for adult life, including knowing where pupils go when they leave?

- How is the school ensuring that it keeps pupils safe from, and building their resilience to, the risks of extremism and radicalisation? What arrangements are in place to ensure that staff understand and are implementing the Prevent duty?

- Are senior leaders including (where appropriate) the chief executive and finance director getting appropriate continuous professional development?

- Does the school have the right staff and the right development and reward arrangements? What is the school's approach to implementation of pay reform and performance related pay? If appropriate, is it compliant with the most up to date version of the School Teachers' Pay and Conditions Document? How is the school planning to ensure it continues to have the right staff?

- Have decisions been made with reference to external evidence, for example, has the Education Endowment Foundation (EEF) Toolkit been used to determine Pupil Premium spending decisions? How will the board know if current approaches are working and how will the impact of decisions and interventions be monitored using appropriate tools such as the EEF DIY Evaluation Guide?

- Are teachers and support staff being used as effectively and efficiently as possible and in line with evidence and guidance?

- To what extent is this a happy school with a positive learning culture? What is the school's record on attendance, behaviour and bullying? Are safeguarding procedures securely in place? What is being done to address any current issues, and how will it know if it is working?

- How good is the school's wider offer to pupils? Is the school offering a good range of sports, arts and voluntary activities? Is school food healthy and popular?

- Is the school encouraging the development of healthy, active lifestyles by using the PE and sport premium for primary schools to fund additional and sustainable improvements to the provision of PE and sport?

- How effectively does the school listen to the views of pupils and parents?

17. The NGA has published 'Knowing your School – Questions for the Board to ask' (content available for NGA members only). The Wellcome Trust's 'Questions for Governors', is a framework to facilitate discussions between governors of both secondary and primary schools and their school leaders on STEM[1] subjects.

18. In line with their third core function, boards should also ask questions about finance and spending – further information on this is available in Section 2.3.

2.3 Overseeing financial performance

19. The board's third core function is to make sure money is well spent. It should do this by ensuring it has at least one governor with specific, relevant skills and experience of financial matters. However, all governors should ideally have a basic understanding of the financial cycle and the legal requirements of the school on accountability and spend. This is important in all schools, but particularly important in MATs or large schools or federations. Their larger budgets make it even more critical that the board not only oversees delivery of the best possible education for pupils, but also provides robust corporate governance to ensure the viability and efficiency of the organisation through effective business and financial planning.

20. Asking the right questions is equally important in relation to money as it is to educational performance. Appropriate questions might include:

- Are resources allocated in line with the school's strategic priorities?

- Does the school have a clear budget forecast, ideally for the next three years, which identifies spending opportunities and risks and sets how these will be mitigated?

- Does the school have sufficient reserves to cover major changes such as re-structuring, and any risks identified in the budget forecast?

- Is the school making best use of its budget, including in relation to planning and delivery of the curriculum?

- Does the school plan its budgets on a bottom up basis driven by curriculum planning (i.e. is the school spending its money in accordance with its priorities) or is the budget set by simply making minor adjustments to last year's budget to ensure there is a surplus?

- Are the school's assets and financial resources being used efficiently?

- How can better value for money be achieved from the budget?

---

[1] Science, Technology, Engineering and Mathematics.

2.4 The importance of objective data

21. The board must have access to objective, high quality and timely data if it is to create robust accountability and know the questions that need to be asked of the school leadership.

22. It is essential that every board has at least one governor with the skills to understand and interpret the full detail of the educational performance and the financial data available. These governors should make sure that the board has a correct understanding of the school's performance and finances. They should identify from the data the issues that need to be discussed and addressed as a priority. Other governors should learn from them and undertake any available training opportunities to improve their confidence and skills in looking at data. While boards may decide to establish a committee to look in detail at performance data, all governors should be able to engage fully with discussions about data in relation to the educational and financial performance of their school. If they cannot, they should undertake appropriate training or development to enable them to do so. This includes MAT boards who should not leave this function solely to LGBs, where they are in place, but should themselves be familiar with and interrogate key performance data.

2.4.1 Sources of education data

23. It is the headteacher's job to provide their board with the information it needs to do its job well. This means they should help the board access the data published by the department and Ofsted. They should also provide whatever management information the board requires to monitor different aspects of life in the school throughout the year. In particular, a board will need to see information relating to the priorities it has identified for improvement. This might include data on:

    - pupil learning and progress;
    - pupil applications, admissions, attendance and exclusions;
    - staff deployment, absence, recruitment, retention, morale and performance; and
    - the quality of teaching.

24. The board, not the headteacher, should determine the scope and format of headteacher's reports. This will mean that the board receives the information it needs in a format that enables it to stay focused on its core strategic functions and not get distracted or overwhelmed by information of secondary importance. As MATs grow, their scale means that they have greater opportunity to employ a central executive team to help them discharge their oversight responsibilities, including by compiling and analysing pupil progress and financial performance data and using a standard template to present data from each school in the MAT.

25. The headteacher and school should not be the only source of information for the board. That would make it hard to hold the headteacher to account properly. Governors need to make sure that at least once a year they see objective national data so that they are empowered to ask pertinent and searching questions. A board can get annual performance data direct from a number of sources.

Ofsted's school performance dashboard

26. Ofsted has published short reports for schools in England to explain the school's performance in a clear and simple way. The reports cover pupils' attainment and progress in core subjects, their attendance, and how well the school is doing for its disadvantaged pupils. They show how well schools are performing compared to national averages and compared to similar schools – those whose pupils had similar attainment when they entered the school. Reports are available at key stages 1, 2 and 4.

27. Governors who are not accustomed to looking at education performance data will find these reports an easy way to understand whether and how their school needs to improve; the reports help governors to raise questions. School and college performance tables and RAISEonline[2] provide detailed information that will help governors scrutinise any issues they find.

School and college performance tables

28. The department collects data about schools and publishes it in performance tables for everyone to see. This helps to ensure that there is sufficient transparency and public accountability for school performance.

29. The performance tables provide information on pupil attainment and progress, school finances, pupil absence and school workforce. They also contain the most recent overall Ofsted judgement on each school and a link to inspection reports.

30. Governors can use performance tables to compare their own school with other local or similar schools to see:

- how well their school is doing against a range of performance measures – including each of the department's 'floor standard' measures on attainment and progress;
- how well a primary school is doing at key stage 2 in reading; writing; grammar, punctuation and spelling; and mathematics;
- how well a secondary school is doing at key stage 4 in terms of the number of pupils achieving 5A*-C (or equivalents) including English and mathematics GCSEs, and percentage of pupils achieving 5+ A*-G grade GCSEs (or equivalent);
- how well a sixth-form is doing in A levels and other level 3 qualifications;
- how attainment and progress compares between different groups of pupils, including disadvantaged pupils, those with English as an Additional Language (EAL), and 'non-mobile' pupils (i.e. those who have been in the school throughout each of the last two years);
- how the school spends its money, shown as £ per pupil to allow comparison between schools of different size; and
- information about people who work at the school, including the number of teachers, teaching assistants, support workers; their average salaries; and the ratio of teachers to pupils.

---

[2] Reporting and Analysis for Improvement through school Self-Evaluation

RAISEonline

31. RAISEonline is a secure web-based system available to governors, schools, and local authorities. Ofsted inspectors also use it to inform their inspections. The system uses the data collected for performance tables, but provides a more detailed analysis. RAISEonline reports use tables, graphs and charts to show the attainment and progress of the school and a wide range of different pupil groups.

32. RAISEonline includes data on pupil attainment, progress, absence, and exclusions. It provides an analysis of the characteristics of pupils, such as their ethnic mix, special educational needs, and level of deprivation. All data are compared to the relevant national average. RAISEonline highlights key strengths and weaknesses. It shows clearly where a difference from the national average is large enough to say with confidence that it is not there by chance, but due to a genuine difference at the school.

33. The RAISEonline summary report signposts the data that governors may want to focus on as their starting point for understanding their school's performance. The summary report does not contain any named pupil data.

34. The inspection dashboard has been created in RAISEonline to support new inspection arrangements from September 2015. The dashboard is a tool showing historic data for inspectors to use when preparing for inspections. It is designed to show at a glance how well previous cohorts demonstrated characteristics of good or better performance. It contains a brief overview of published data for the last three years using clear visual displays that are quick to interpret.

35. Legislation[3] ensures that all governors are entitled to access the RAISEonline system for their school, but it is up to the headteacher or the school's RAISEonline administrator to determine what level of data they want to share. The school's administrator can provide them with a 'governor' account, which allows access to the RAISEonline summary report only. Schools are not required to provide access to the interactive data contained within the RAISEonline system. Some schools may do so by giving governors a 'school' user account. A summary of access rights is available in the RAISEonline library in the 'Frequently asked questions' folder.

36. Governors who lead on understanding and scrutinising attainment data should see and analyse the full RAISEonline summary report. For other governors, less detail may suffice but it is important that all governors see some form of summary of key RAISEonline data for their school, and are able to identify the strengths and weaknesses of the school. All governors must be able to engage in a discussion about RAISEonline or equivalent data and, if not, should attend a course to enable them to do so.

---

[3] Regulation 3(5)(e) of The Education (Individual Pupil Information) (Prescribed Persons) (England) Regulations 2009.

37. Governors can use RAISEonline to look into their school's performance. They can look at the high-level figures. They can also drill down for example into the performance of different pupil groups. In particular, governors can use it to identify priorities for improvement in the light of:

   • the attainment of different groups of pupils and in different subjects, and how this compares to national 'floor standards' for key stage 2 and key stage 4;

   • the progress made by different groups of pupils and in different subjects, and how this compares to 'expected progress' measures; and

   • the progress made by pupils compared to all pupils nationally and pupils with similar prior attainment.

38. The NGA has published guides to help governors get the most out of the data in RAISEonline. Free training workshops for governors on RAISEonline are available through NCTL licensees.

Other sources of education data

39. In addition to the government data sources outlined above, there is a growing range of products from third parties that aim to meet boards' data needs. Many of these draw, at least in part, on the department's data. Bearing in mind that RAISEonline contains the data that Ofsted inspectors use, it is for boards to choose which works best for them. Options include products developed by some local authorities as well as tools such as the Fischer Family Trust's Governor Dashboard, developed in partnership with the NGA and the Wellcome Trust.

2.4.2 Sources of financial data

40. The department provides a range of financial information about maintained schools and academies. EFA's toolkit for schools provides information for academy trusts about the support available to improve efficiency, including a new financial benchmarking website. Boards can use this information to compare spending against that of similar schools. Benchmarking financial information in this way helps boards to question whether resources could be used more efficiently. For example:

   • Are other schools buying things cheaper or getting better results with less spending per pupil?

   • If the cost of energy seems high compared to similar schools, are there opportunities for investment in energy-saving devices to reduce the cost?

   • If spend on learning resources seems high compared to similar schools, are there opportunities for collaborating with other local schools to bring costs down?

   • If your spending on staffing is higher than other similar schools, are these schools achieving more in terms of attainment? If so what might be learnt from them about how they deploy their workforce?

   • If the spend on teaching assistants is higher than other schools, are Governors sure that they are being used effectively and efficiently to support pupil outcomes?

41. Financial requirements on academy trusts are set out in EFA's 'Academies Financial Handbook' and in their funding agreement. Academies and their auditors should also read the 'Academies Accounts Direction', when preparing and auditing annual reports and financial statements.

42. There is a wide range of information sources and tools available to help schools secure the best value for money. ASCL have published their Basic tenets of sound financial planning to ensure that your school is running at maximum efficiency.

43. Further guidance and links to organisations that are able to provide support are available on GOV.UK.

44. Section 12 details boards' financial responsibilities, as well as information on the dedicated schools grant and pupil premium.

2.4.3 School visits

45. Governors need to know their school if accountability is going to be robust and their vision for the school is to be achieved. Many governors find that visiting, particularly during the day, is a helpful way to find out more about the school. Through pre-arranged visits that have a clear focus, governors can see for themselves whether the school is implementing their policies and improvement plans and how they are working in practice. Visits also provide an opportunity to talk with pupils, staff and parents to gather their views, though are unlikely to be sufficient for these purposes.

46. Governors are not inspectors and it is not their role to assess the quality or method of teaching or extent of learning. They are also not school managers and should make sure they do not interfere in the day-to-day running of the school. Both are the role of the headteacher. If governors wish to spend time within a classroom, they need to be very clear why they are doing so.

Section 3 – People

1. The effectiveness of a board depends on the quality of its people and how they work together and with school leaders. This section explains the principles underpinning how the board must be constituted.

3.1 Constitution and membership of the board

2. While boards in some schools have more flexibility than in others, all boards have a choice about how they are constituted. It is the constitution of the board that determines how many and what type of people govern the school.

3. All boards of maintained schools, academies and MATs should be tightly focused and no larger than they need to be to have all the necessary skills to carry out their functions effectively, with every member actively contributing relevant skills and experience. In general, the department believes that smaller boards are more likely to be cohesive and dynamic, and able to act more decisively. Boards cannot afford to carry passengers.

4. The need for boards to establish committees, or panels, for exclusions or disciplinary matters, does not necessitate in itself a large board. Committees or panels can be established specifically for these purposes, to which non-board members may be appointed, and/or a committee may be established as a joint committee with another school.

5. The membership of the board should focus on skills, and the primary consideration in the appointment and election of new governors should be acquiring the skills and experience the board needs to be effective. Boards should therefore develop a skills-based set of criteria for governor selection and recruitment which can also be used to inform ongoing self-evaluation and governor training. For maintained schools, the School Governance (Constitution) (England) Regulations 2012 require all appointed governors to have the skills required to contribute to effective governance and the success of the school.

6. Meaningful and effective engagement with parents, staff and the wider community is vital, and not achieved by the presence of various categories of governor on the board. Governors must govern in the best interest of pupils; it is not their role to represent a stakeholder group. Stakeholder engagement is an important, but distinct, activity for which boards will need to assure themselves that appropriate structures and arrangements are in place. Governors themselves should seek to assist their school to build relationships with business and other employers, in order to enhance the education and raise the aspirations of pupils.

7. Boards should carry out regular audits of governors' skills in the light of the skills and competences they need, and actively seek to address any gaps they identify – through either recruitment or training as discussed further below. They should also reflect regularly on whether they have the right overall balance of people and skills, and consider the benefits that might result from restructuring the board's constitution and membership. 'A Possible Road Map for Governing Board Reconstitution' aims to help boards with the practicalities of how to approach the process of reconstitution.

8. As highlighted in statutory guidance for maintained schools on the constitution of the board (the principles of which may also be of interest to academies), it is for whoever is appointing the governor to be confident that they have the necessary skills, including the willingness and ability to learn and develop as a governor. To make an informed decision on the matter an interview or detailed discussion will need to take place with each prospective candidate, with references (oral or written) taken as necessary and appropriate. Boards and others responsible for nominating or appointing governors should make use of all available channels to identify suitable governors. Where governors are elected, every effort should be made to inform the electorate about the role of a governor and the specific skills the board requires and the extent to which candidates possess these.

9. The department recognises that there are people who have the skill and the time to serve effectively on a number of boards, and does not want to restrict their ability to do so. However, where a prospective governor is already a governor of another school or MAT, the chair of the board, should speak to the chair of the other board to discuss both the skills of the individual and, where appropriate, their capacity to serve effectively on an additional board. It is likely that only in exceptional circumstances will an individual have the capacity to serve effectively on more than two boards – but this is rightly a matter for the board and/or other appointing body to decide.

10. It is essential that boards recruit and develop governors with the skills to deliver their core functions effectively. However, it is equally important to emphasise that the skills required are those to oversee the success of the school, not to do the school's job for it. For example, a governor with financial expertise should use their skills to scrutinise the school's accounts, not to help prepare them. If a governor does possess skills that the school wishes to utilise on a pro bono basis, then it is important that this is considered separately from their role in governance, and steps should be taken to minimise conflicts of interest and ensure that this does not blur lines of accountability.

11. With effective succession planning in place, it can be beneficial for strong governors and chairs in particular to move on to another school after a reasonable time (e.g. two terms of office). This can help to share expertise across the system and prevent boards stagnating or individual governors gaining too much power and influence solely through their length of service.

12. While it is essential to build a strong and cohesive non-executive team, the most robust boards welcome and thrive on having a sufficiently diverse range of viewpoints – since open debate leads to good decisions in the interests of the whole school community. While noting the role of foundation governors in a faith-designated school, boards should be alert to the risk of becoming dominated by one particular mind-set or strand of opinion, whether related to faith or otherwise. Having some members who have no close ties with the school can help ensure that the board has sufficient internal challenge to how they carry out their strategic functions.

13. Effective boards think carefully about how they are organised. This includes thinking about whether and how to use their powers to delegate functions and decisions to committees or individual governors. Boards may decide to task individual governors to take an interest in a specific area, such as SEN, safeguarding or health and safety – although there is no statutory requirement for them to do so. There are many different models and boards are best placed to decide for themselves what will work best in their own circumstances.

14. Boards are legally responsible for the conduct of the school. However, individual governors are generally protected from personal liability. Provided they act honestly, reasonably and in good faith, any liability will fall on the board even if it exceeds its powers, rather than on individual members.

3.2 The kind of people the board needs

15. Boards must have a keen understanding of the skills they need to deliver effective governance. The specific skills that a board needs to meet its particular challenges will vary. It is therefore for the board and other appointing persons to determine in their own opinion what these skills are and be satisfied that people they appoint possess them. Relevant skills may include important personal attributes, qualities and capabilities, such as the ability and willingness to learn and develop new skills.

16. All governors need a strong commitment to the role and to improving outcomes for children; the inquisitiveness to question and analyse; and the willingness to learn. They need good inter-personal skills, appropriate levels of literacy in English (unless a board is prepared to make special arrangements), and sufficient numeracy skills to understand basic data. Foundation governors are selected for their skills as well as their ability to secure the character and ethos of the school.

17. Effective boards seek to secure or develop within their membership as a whole expertise and experience in analysing performance data, in budgeting and driving financial efficiency, and in performance management and employment issues, including grievances. They seek to recruit and/or develop governors with the skills to work constructively in committees, chair meetings and to lead the board.

18. Boards have a responsibility to fill governor vacancies as soon as possible. In filling vacancies, boards and others responsible for nominating or appointing governors should make use of all available channels to identify suitable governors – further details on the help available from Academy Ambassadors, SGOSS Governors for Schools, and the Education & Employers Taskforce as well as information about the Inspiring Governors Alliance can be found in Section 14.

19. All trustees of academies must by DBS checked, and the department has recently consulted on introducing the same requirement for governors of maintained schools – details on DBS checks in schools are within the statutory guidance Keeping children safe in education.

Time off work

20. People from the world of work often bring important transferable skills to the board. Serving as a governor also helps employees develop board-level skills and experience that they can take back into the workplace that they may not otherwise develop until much later in their careers. The learning and development benefits are therefore significant and more than compensate for the flexibility and time off that staff may need to fulfil their governor duties. The Confederation of British Industry (CBI) has stated clearly that it sees a robust business case for more employers supporting their staff to volunteer as governors[4].

21. By law, employers must give employees who are school governors in maintained schools 'reasonable time off' to carry out their duties[5]. The employee and employer must agree on what is 'reasonable time off'. Employers may give time off with pay but do not have to do so. This is for discussion between the employee and the employer. Guidance on time off for public duties is available.

22. If the employee and employer cannot agree on any of these questions, either of them can ask for help from the Advisory Conciliation and Arbitration Service (ACAS), which will try to settle any differences informally. An employee who is still not satisfied may complain to an Employment Tribunal.

3.3 Induction and ongoing training and development

23. Boards are responsible for identifying and securing the induction and other ongoing training and development governors need. They should set aside a budget for this purpose.

24. As part of induction and continuous development, effective boards encourage every governor, especially those new to the role, to make the most of the resources and guidance available to develop their knowledge and skills. Examples of some of the support and resources available are listed within Section 14.

25. Good boards set out clearly what they expect of their governors, particularly when they first join. The board's code of conduct should set an ethos of professionalism and high expectations of governors, including an expectation that they undertake whatever training or development activity is needed to fill any gaps in the skills they have to contribute to effective governance. Importantly, this includes their ability to understand and interpret educational and financial performance data. All governors should be able to engage fully with discussions on these matters and if they cannot, they should undertake appropriate training or development to enable them to do so.

26. Boards should consider giving the vice-chair or another governor a specific responsibility for ensuring every governor develops the skills they need to be effective. Rather than simply track governors' attendance at training courses, with administrative support from the clerk, this governor would be responsible for ensuring that every new and existing governor develops their

---

[4] CBI Report: Leading the Way – Improving School Governance and Leadership

[5] Section 50 of the Employment Rights Act 1996

skills to make an active and valuable contribution to the work of the board. Any persistent skills gaps across the board or for individual governors should be brought to the attention of the chair.

27. If, in the view of the board, a governor fails persistently to undertake the training of development they need, then they should consider suspending the governor on the grounds that they will be in breach of the board's code of conduct and may bring the board or the office of a governor into disrepute.

28. Boards should have succession plans in place and develop future leaders by identifying and nurturing talent and sharing responsibility.

3.4 Transparency

29. Governors hold an important public office and their identity should be known to their school and wider communities. In the interests of transparency, all boards should publish on their school website up-to-date details of their governance arrangements in a readily accessible format[6]. Further detail of the information that should be published is available in the statutory guidance Constitution of governing bodies of maintained schools and in the Academies Financial Handbook.

---

[6] Readily accessible means that the information should be on a webpage without the need to download or open a separate document.

Section 4 – Structures

1. This section explains the specific structures of governance for academies and maintained schools, starting with further discussion on the benefits of governing a group of schools.

4.1 Multi-school governance structures

2. As highlighted in Section 1, governance structures that span more than one school create an opportunity for higher quality governance. The boards of maintained school federations and the boards of multi-academy trusts have a more strategic perspective and the ability to compare and contrast between schools. They also create the opportunity for the skills of high calibre people to be brought to bear in overseeing more schools to the benefit of more pupils.

3. Governing a group of schools through a single board also creates the condition for fully realising the sustained benefits of school-to-school collaboration, which include:

    *   A richer and wider curriculum – including through the ability to recruit and deploy more specialist staff, such as subject specialists or faculty heads;
    *   Better professional development and career progression opportunities for staff, and better retention of key staff as a result;
    *   Bigger leadership challenges for middle and senior leaders, while also easing the overall leadership challenge through more supported leadership roles;
    *   Financial efficiency – through shared procurement;
    *   Economies of scale – that make employing specialist finance directors and business managers with vital skills more feasible; and
    *   Ultimately, better prospects for pupils through greater professional accountability and the roll out of consistent proven pedagogies.

4. Many governors, like headteachers and parents, can be passionate and committed to their school. However, governing is about putting the interests of pupils before adults and boards should set aside issues of control and school identity to consider objectively the governance structures that would most benefit current and future pupils.

4.2 The governance structure of academies

5. An academy trust is a charitable company limited by guarantee. A standalone academy trust is a single legal entity responsible for one academy that has its own articles of association and funding agreement with the Secretary of State. A multi-academy trust is also a single legal entity with its own articles of association and master funding agreement with the Secretary of State. A MAT is established to take responsibility for more than one academy. Each academy within a MAT has its own supplemental funding agreement. Every free school, studio school and university technical college is run by an academy trust.

4.2.1 Members and trustees

6. All academy trusts have at least two layers of governance:

   - Members – who have ultimate responsibility for the trust achieving its charitable objectives. They sign off the articles of association and have power to appoint and remove the trustees.

   - Trustees – who collectively as the board of trustees deliver the three core functions common to school governance. The trustees must also ensure compliance with company and charity law and with the trust's funding agreement with the Secretary of State.

Members

7. Academy trusts must have at least three members, although the department encourages trusts to have at least five members in total, as this:

   - ensures enough members can take decisions via special resolution (which requires 75% of members to agree) without requiring unanimity; and

   - facilitates majority decisions being taken by ordinary resolution (which requires a majority of members to agree).

8. Particularly in MATs given the breadth of their responsibilities, the most robust governance structures will have at least some distinction between the individuals who are members and those who are trustees. This enables members who are independent of the trustees to provide challenge and scrutiny to the board. If there is a risk that members who are trustees will dominate the board, a flat structure may be preferable in which all trustees are members – though the department's preference would still be for there to be some members who are not trustees.

9. A lead sponsor will have majority control of the academy trust by having the right to appoint the majority of its members. Likewise, the minority or majority control of the church in a voluntary controlled or voluntary aided school is retained on conversion to academy status through minority or majority control over the appointment of members of the trust – who in turn appoint the majority of the trustees.

10. Employees of the trust cannot be appointed as members.

Trustees

11. The constitution of the board of trustees is set out in each trust's own articles of association. Academy trusts have almost complete flexibility to design the constitution of their board of trustees as they see fit in order to ensure it has the necessary skills and capacity to carry out its functions effectively. There are very few requirements relating to the constitution of the board of trustees in the department's model articles of association:

    - The board must include at least two elected parent trustees – in a MAT the parents can be at board level or on each LGB (explained further below).

    - No more than one third of the board can be employees of the trust.

- No more than 19.9 per cent of the board can be local authority associated – i.e. people employed by a local authority (including teachers and headteachers of LA maintained schools) or people who are or have been within the last four years a member of a local authority, where that local authority has a responsibility for education or is a district or parish council where there is a land or other commercial relationship with the trust; and

- For university technical colleges there is a requirement that nominees of the employer and university sponsors must together form the majority on the board of trustees.

12. Our model articles give members the decision on whether to appoint the principal as a trustee, if he/she is willing to be. The principal or any other employee who is appointed as a trustee is appointed on the basis that their role as trustees is dependent on their employment by the trust and that if they leave the trust, they cease to be a trustee.

13. The board is able to remove from office any trustee that they have appointed. In addition members have the power[7] to remove any trustee irrespective of whether the individual was appointed or elected to the board.

14. Academy trusts of newly converted schools are required to set out in the governance statement, submitted with their first audited accounts, what they have done to review and develop their governance structure and composition of the board of trustees. The department recommends that the trust continue this practice in each subsequent year.

15. Free school proposer groups should design and populate strong governance structures and reporting arrangements during the pre-opening period that will drive improvement in their free school once it opens. The departmental advice, Free schools – Pre-opening proposer group guidance, sets out everything the proposer group need to put in place strong governance arrangements.

4.2.2 Multi-academy trusts

16. A MAT board is accountable for all of the academies within the trust. However, it can choose to delegate governance functions to local governing bodies or LGBs. LGBs may govern one academy or they may govern more than one academy. Particularly in a large MAT, the board may decide to appoint a committee to oversee a group of LGBs, for example as a regional cluster. Both committees and LGBs are made up of people that the MAT board appoints – this may include MAT trustees but can be anyone that the board selects for their skills. Committee members and local governors are not trustees of the MAT unless they also sit on the MAT board itself.

17. It is the decision of the trustees about which, if any, governance functions they delegate to LGBs or other committees. LGBs with no delegated governance functions are wholly advisory. Many MATs delegate responsibilities in proportion to the strength of individual academies and the skills and expertise of their local governors – for example by increasing levels of delegation as initially weak schools improve. Boards considering joining a MAT should ensure they understand the range of governance functions, if any, that would be delegated to them

---

[7] Section 282 of the Companies Act 2006

as an LGB by the MAT board; and understand that the board will have full control over the membership of the LGB that they become.

18. The Academies Financial Handbook requires all academies and MATs to publish on their website their scheme of delegation for governance functions. This should set out in a clear and concise format the structure and remit of the members and of the board of trustees, its committees and LGBs – including details of which governance functions have been delegated and which remain with the trust board. All individuals involved in the governance of a MAT should know who the trustees are and understand clearly what functions have been delegated by the board to LGBs or other committees.

19. As they grow, MAT boards have the opportunity to expand their central executive team as means of exercising their responsibilities of oversight. However, as individual school principals become line managed by, for example, a chief executive, there is a risk of duplication or confusion between the role of the chief executive and the LGB in holding the school principal to account. MATs need to consider carefully and be clear about how they will exercise their governance and oversight through both executive and non-executive channels and how the two fit together.

20. MATs can also use their executive team to oversee finances. Many MAT boards tell us that in hindsight they would have appointed a finance director earlier in their growth. A dedicated finance director is essential to overseeing the efficient and effective use of the MAT's resources for the benefit of pupils, and that systems for financial planning and control are appropriate and sufficient.

21. As set out in Section 1, in order to transition successfully from a single academy into a small MAT, and onward into a large MAT, the board should commission a robust independent external review of its effectiveness and readiness for growth. The board of a single school might try to develop its existing governance model to form a small MAT of two or three schools, but growth beyond three schools usually represents the first real need to overhaul governance arrangements. Likewise the governance structures of a small MAT will start to become stretched at around 6-7 schools and by 10 a further overhaul will be needed.

22. More information and case studies on MAT governance are available on GOV.UK.

4.3 The governance structure of maintained schools

4.3.1 Single maintained schools

23. All maintained school boards must be constituted under the 2012 Constitution Regulations. Statutory guidance on these regulations, Constitution of governing bodies of maintained schools, is available on GOV.UK.

24. These regulations provide that the minimum size of the board is seven members and the board must include:

    - at least two parent governors – elected where possible, otherwise appointed;
    - the headteacher, unless the headteacher decides not to be a governor;
    - only one elected staff governor;
    - only one local authority governor; nominated by the LA, appointed by the board, and
    - where appropriate, foundation governors – appointed by the relevant foundation, or partnership governors – nominated by the appropriate religious body (where the school has a religious character) or by parents or the local community and appointed by the board as specified in the regulations.

25. The board may appoint as many additional co-opted governors as it considers necessary. The number of co-opted governors who are eligible to be elected or appointed as staff governors must not (when added to the one staff governor and the headteacher) exceed one-third of the total membership of the board. The term of office for each category of governor is decided by the board and set out in the instrument of government. Additionally, boards may decide to adopt the flexibility for those appointing governors to decide the term of office of each individual governor to be between 1 and 4 years. This will only apply to newly appointed governors and would not affect the terms of office of existing governors.

26. For local authority governor appointments, a board should make clear its eligibility criteria including its expectations of the credentials and skills prospective candidates should possess. Local authorities must then make every effort to understand the board's requirements in order to identify and nominate suitable candidates. It is for the board to decide whether the local authority nominee meets any stated eligibility criteria and, if it chooses to reject the candidate on that basis, to explain their decision to the local authority.

27. Once appointed, local authority governors must govern in the interests of the school and not represent or advocate for the political or other interests of the local authority; it is unacceptable practice to link the right to nominate local authority governors to the local balance of political power.

28. The board can appoint associate members to serve on one or more committees of the board. Associate members can attend full board meetings but may be excluded from any part of a meeting where the business being considered concerns a member of school staff or an individual pupil. They are appointed for a period of between one and four years and can be reappointed at the end of their term of office. Associate members are not governors and they are not recorded in the instrument of government.

29. The definition of associate member is wide and pupils, school staff and people who want to contribute specifically on issues related to their area of expertise (for instance, finance) can be appointed as associate members.

30. The constitution of all boards is set out in their instrument of government[8]. The board drafts the instrument and submits it to the local authority. Before the board submits the draft instrument to the local authority, it must be approved by any foundation governors and, where relevant, any trustees and/or the appropriate religious body or appointing authority. The local authority must check if the draft instrument complies with the legal requirements, including the relevant guiding principles for the constitution of boards. If the instrument complies with the legal requirements, the local authority will 'make' the instrument. The instrument can be reviewed and changed at any time.

31. A school may have more governors in a particular category than is provided for in its instrument of government. This situation could arise if a board has decided to reconstitute and reduce in size but sufficient resignations are not forthcoming for the remaining members to fit within the new structure. Further guidance on managing this process is available in statutory guidance.

32. The board, and where applicable other appointing bodies, are able to remove any governor that they have appointed. Elected governors cannot be removed from office. Further detail on the procedure for removing governors from office is available in statutory guidance.

4.3.2 The governance structures of maintained school federations

33. Federation creates a single board to govern more than one maintained school. Schools in federations continue to be individual schools, keeping their existing category, character and legal identity, but have their governance provided by the same board. Admission to each school continues to be determined by the appropriate admissions authority. The board of the federation will receive individual budgets for each of the federated schools, and can pool these budgets to use across the schools in the federation as it sees fit. Staff may also be employed at the federation level to enable flexible deployment between schools.

34. A board's decision to federate must follow a prescribed process, which is detailed in the School Governance (Federations) Regulations 2012. A prescribed process must also be followed when an individual school wishes to leave a federation or where the federation board decides to dissolve the federation; these processes are also detailed in the federation regulations.

35. The Regulations require the board of all federations to have at least seven members, including:

   - one parent governor in respect of each school in the federation;
   - the headteacher of each federated school (or the executive headteacher of the federation, if there is one) unless they resign as a governor;
   - one elected staff governor; and
   - one local authority governor – nominated by the LA and appointed by the board.

---

[8] This includes community, community special, foundation (including qualifying foundation schools, foundation schools with and foundation schools without a foundation), foundation special, voluntary-aided (VA), voluntary-controlled (VC) and maintained nursery schools.

36. In addition, federations comprising foundation and voluntary schools are required to have foundation or partnership governors. The statutory guidance, Constitution of governing bodies of maintained schools, is available.

37. It is possible that each school within a federation will have its own headteacher. In these circumstances, each headteacher will be entitled to a place on the board. To be a headteacher the person must be being paid at the appropriate pay scale and be performing the duties in the school, which the board has conferred upon the headteacher through the School Teachers' Pay and Conditions Document. Alternatively, the federation may have a single executive headteacher that sits on the board.

38. The 2012 Federations Regulations mirror the categories and eligibility criteria set out in the 2012 Constitution Regulations.

39. The board may also appoint as many co-opted governors as they consider necessary, but in doing so, it must take into account the additional requirement for federations comprising foundation and voluntary schools where there may be a requirement to have a majority of foundation governors. The total number of co-opted governors who are also eligible to be elected or appointed as staff governors (when counted with the staff governor and the headteacher/s) must not exceed one third of the total membership of the board of the federation.

40. We have recently consulted on reducing the requirement for parent governors from one per school to two, and only two, with the proposed changes expected to come into force from September 2016.

4.4 School collaboration

41. Collaboration is when schools work together without a single over-arching governance structure.

4.4.1 Umbrella Trusts

42. Some academies have created an 'umbrella trust' as a vehicle for collaboration. This means that while the academies remain separate charitable trusts with their own articles and funding agreement with the Secretary of State, they create an additional charitable trust with functions that reflect their mutual interests. This often involves the individual academies ceding powers of oversight, intervention or governance to the umbrella trust. The department's preference is for groups of schools or academies intending to collaborate to form a multi-academy trust in which there is robust shared governance arrangements and clear lines of accountability[9].

---

[9] In relation to Church of England academies, while Diocesan Boards of Education have often established what they also call umbrella trusts to be the corporate member of an academy trust or MAT on behalf of the Diocesan Board of Education, they are not part of the governance structure and have no decision-making powers. Umbrella trusts of this type are normally charitable companies and so may have other roles outside the governance structure of the academy trust.

4.4.2 Maintained school collaboration

43. Maintained schools may collaborate formally with other maintained schools, hold joint board meetings and form joint committees[10]. The School Governance (Collaboration) (England) Regulations 2003 leave much of the detailed arrangements to the schools concerned. They allow two or more boards to arrange for any of their functions to be carried out jointly, as well as allowing those functions to be delegated to a joint committee. The specific procedures (on clerking and membership of committees, for example) generally mirror those for individual schools. Individual boards retain legal responsibility and corporate liability for all decisions made on their behalf. Boards must therefore make sure that they receive regular reports, including signed minutes, from any joint committees they agree to establish.

44. Maintained schools may also enter into collaborative arrangements with FE colleges using joint committees[11].

4.4.3 Collaboration between academies and maintained schools

45. While the Collaboration Regulations do not permit maintained schools to share governance arrangements and form formal joint committees with academies, they may collaborate informally. For example, a joint committee may be established which is purely advisory in nature, making recommendations to the boards of both schools who retain decision making powers. Alternatively, the committee may be established with parallel dual identities – complying with both the requirements of maintained school regulations and the legal framework for academies.

---

[10] Section 26 of the Education Act 2002.

[11] The Collaboration Arrangements (Maintained Schools and Further Education Bodies) (England) Regulations 2007.

◗ SCHOLASTIC

Section 5 – Ways of Working

1. Boards are generally best placed to decide how they can best work effectively in the light of their own local circumstances. There are, however, some key general principles and some specific basic rules to ensure a minimum level of effectiveness.

2. Any rules on how boards of academies must operate will be set out in their articles of association, the funding agreement and within the Academies Financial Handbook.

3. The School Governance (Roles, Procedures and Allowances) (England) Regulations 2013 for maintained schools and the management committees of pupil referral units cover board procedures, terms of reference and governors' allowances.

5.1 Conduct

4. Governors should be mindful that in exercising all their functions, they must act with integrity, objectivity and honesty and in the best interests of the school; and be open about the decisions they make and the actions they take and be prepared to explain their decisions and actions to interested parties. This is required in maintained schools by legislation[12].

5. Similarly, governors should be aware of and accept the seven principles of public life, as set out by Lord Nolan and applying to anyone, locally and nationally, who is elected or appointed as a public office-holder. They are selflessness, integrity, objectivity, accountability, openness, honesty and leadership.

6. A code of conduct should be maintained and communicated to all prospective governors to set clear expectations of the governors' role and behaviour. Explicit agreement to the code of conduct will mean there is a common reference point should any difficulties arise in the future. The NGA Model Code of Conduct aims to helps boards draft a code of conduct which sets out the purpose of the board and describes the appropriate relationship between individual governors, the whole board and the leadership team of the school.

5.2 Having regard to the views of parents

7. All boards should assure themselves that mechanisms are in place to engage meaningfully with parents and enable all parents to put forward their views at key points in their child's education. The board should be able to demonstrate the methods used to seek the views of parents and how those views have influenced their decision making[13].

---

[12] The School Governance (Roles, Procedures and Allowances) (England) Regulations 2013

[13] For maintained schools, this is a statutory duty as set out in Section 21(7) of the Education Act 2002 (as inserted by section 38 of the Education and Inspections Act. 2006.

5.3 Equality

8. The Equality Act 2010 applies to all schools in their role as employers, as providers of education to the pupils in their care and as providers of a service or public function. The board or academy trust is responsible for compliance with the public sector equality duties of the Act and the specific education sections (part 4) for school pupils.

9. The Equality Act's general and specific public sector equality duties mean that schools must:
   - have due regard to the need to eliminate discrimination;
   - advance equality of opportunity and foster good relations across all characteristics; and
   - publish equality objectives and information demonstrating how they are doing this.

10. The Equality and Human Rights Commission (EHRC) can enforce this duty by issuing a compliance notice to order a school to meet the duty within a certain timescale. The departmental advice on the Equality Act 2010 gives detailed information for schools.

11. Boards should make sure that their school complies with all aspects of discrimination law. The best way to do this is to ensure that they apply the principles of fairness and equality in everything that the school does. Schools with a religious character have legitimate exemptions.

12. Discrimination claims are heard in the county court, with the exception of pupil disability claims in schools and employment claims, which are both heard in specific tribunals.

5.4 Charitable and corporate duties

13. Academy trustees are charity trustees. As such, they must comply with the following duties under charity law:
   - ensure the charity is carrying out its purposes for the public benefit;
   - comply with the charity's governing document and the law;
   - act in the charity's best interests;
   - manage the charity's resources responsibly;
   - act with reasonable care and skill; and
   - ensure the charity is accountable

14. These requirements are reflected in the funding agreement and the Academies Financial Handbook. More information on the role of a charity trustee is available on the Charity Commission's website (CC3).

15. Academy trustees must also comply with their statutory duties as company directors, which are set out in sections 170 to 177 of the Companies Act 2006. In practical terms, all trustees need to be familiar with their academy's articles of association as well as their statutory duties under the Companies Act, which comprise the duties to:
   - act within their powers;
   - promote the success of the company;

- exercise independent judgment;
- exercise reasonable care, skill and diligence;
- avoid conflicts of interest;
- not to accept benefits from third parties; and
- declare any interest in proposed transactions or arrangements.

16. The duties of a company director and charitable trustee should not put anyone off from serving as an academy trustee as the core duties of the role are very similar to those of a maintained school governor.

5.5 Dealing with complaints

17. The boards of all schools have a duty to consider complaints about the school and any community facilities or services that it provides[14].

18. Academies must make available on request a procedure for dealing with complaints. The expectation is that this should be published online. For complaints from parents of pupils, this procedure must comply with The Education (Independent School Standards) Regulations 2014.

19. An individual can complain to the Secretary of State for Education if they believe that a board is acting 'unreasonably', or is failing to carry out its statutory duties properly[15]. The Education Funding Agency (EFA) handles complaints about academies on behalf of the Secretary of State.

20. Guidance on making a complaint about a school gives detailed information about the role of the Secretary of State and EFA in the complaints process. Guidance to help schools draw up a complaints procedure is available.

5.6 Whistleblowing

21. All schools and academy trusts should have appropriate procedures in place for whistleblowing. The board need to ensure that staff and governors alike are aware of to whom they can report their concerns, and the way in which such concerns will be managed.

22. The whistleblowing charity, Public Concern at Work (PCAW), provides support for organisations and confidential independent advice to employees about wrongdoing in the workplace. You can contact PCAW at:

- Tel: 020 7404 6609
Email: services@pcaw.co.uk
UK advice line: whistle@pcaw.org.uk

23. The whistleblowing page on GOV.UK provides further information on the areas for which whistleblowing arrangements should cover.

---

[14] Section 29 of the Education Act 2002. For academies and independent schools – Education (Independent School Standards) Regulations 2014.

[15] Sections 496 and 497 of the Education Act 1996.

Section 6 – Education

6.1 The national curriculum

1. The law[16] says that the school curriculum should be balanced and broadly based, and should:

   - promote the spiritual, moral, cultural, mental and physical development of pupils at the school and of society; and

   - prepare pupils at the school for the opportunities, responsibilities and experiences of later life.

2. Responsibility for the curriculum in state schools is shared between the headteacher, the board and (to a limited extent) local authorities. The curriculum for maintained schools must include the national curriculum. The national curriculum sets out the subjects and associated programmes of study that must be taught at each key stage. Academies do not have to follow the national curriculum but they are bound by their funding agreement to teach a broad and balanced curriculum to the age of 16. This must include English, mathematics and science in mainstream academies. Alternative provision academies are not required to teach science.

3. Boards in maintained schools should reassure themselves that:

   - enough teaching time is provided for pupils to cover the national curriculum and other statutory requirements;

   - the relevant assessment arrangements are implemented (see Section 6.6);

   - all courses provided for all pupils below the age of 19 that lead to qualifications such as GCSEs and A levels, are approved by the Secretary of State.

4. The statutory requirements for each subject within the national curriculum for primary and secondary schools are available.

5. The majority of the new national curriculum was introduced in September 2014; English, mathematics and science came into force for years 2 and 6 in September 2015. The English and mathematics curriculum for key stage 4 were phased in from September 2015, and science for key stage 4 will be phased in from September 2016, alongside the timetable for introducing new GCSEs in these subjects.

6. There is no longer a duty on maintained schools to prepare a policy for the school curriculum. If schools do choose to adopt such a policy, it should be broad; it does not need to be a detailed map of all secular curriculum activities.

6.1.1 Study programmes post-16

7. The 16-19 study programmes:

   - aid progression to a higher level than students' prior attainment;

   - include substantial qualifications that provide a recognised route into employment, or higher education;

---

[16] Section 78 of the Education Act 2002

- require students to work towards GCSE A*-C grade in mathematics and English; and
- provide genuine work experience to help students get the experience and skills they will need for future work or education.

8. Funding is per student rather than per qualification. This allows for more innovation and flexibility to meet the needs of all students, including those with learning difficulties and/or disabilities. The EFA has published information about the new funding formula.

6.1.2 Cultural Education

9. It is a legal requirement for both maintained schools and academies to promote the cultural development of their pupils through the spiritual, moral, cultural, mental and physical development education requirements. Cultural education forms an important part of a broad and balanced curriculum, and children and young people should be provided with an engaging variety of cultural experiences throughout their time at school.

10. The policy paper 'Cultural Education' sets out the department's plan for England and provides an overview of some of the programmes and opportunities open to schools and teachers to give all children access to a high-quality cultural education.

11. Appendix A outlines the minimum level of cultural education that a child should expect to receive during his or her schooling as a whole. While voluntary, this would provide a benchmark for a board to reflect on its school cultural provision.

12. There is also a legal requirement placed on maintained schools to provide music and art and design as part of their curriculum for all pupils aged 5 to 14; drama is also present within the national curriculum, and dance is a statutory element of the PE programmes of study.

6.1.3 Sex and relationship education

13. All maintained schools providing secondary education must provide sex education as part of the basic school curriculum. This includes education about HIV and AIDS and other sexually transmitted diseases. All maintained schools must teach human growth and reproduction as set out in the statutory national curriculum for science. Headteachers and governors must make sure that sex education has due regard to moral considerations and the importance of family life.

14. Boards and headteachers of maintained schools providing primary education must decide whether sex education, beyond that set out in the statutory national curriculum for science should be included in their school's curriculum. If so, they must decide what it should consist of and how it should be organised, and keep a record of their decisions.

15. All boards should reassure themselves that the school has a written statement of the policy they adopt on sex education and make it available to parents. All schools providing sex education, including academies through their funding agreements, must have regard to statutory guidance.

16. The PSHE[17] Association has published the advice Sex and relationships education (SRE) for the 21st century to supplement statutory guidance.

6.1.4 Physical Education and Sport

17. A high-quality physical education curriculum inspires all pupils to succeed and excel in competitive sport and other physically demanding activities. It should provide opportunities for pupils to become physically confident in a way which supports their health and fitness. Opportunities to compete in sport and other activities build character and help to embed values such as fairness and respect.

18. All boards should be aware of the PE and sport premium for primary schools. The premium must be used to fund additional and sustainable improvements to the provision of PE and sport, for the benefit of primary-aged pupils, in the 2015 to 2016 academic year, to encourage the development of healthy, active lifestyles. Guidance on how much PE and sport premium funding primary schools receive and advice on how to spend it has been published.

6.1.5 Religious education

19. All state-funded schools must teach religious education (RE). Maintained schools without a religious character should follow their locally agreed syllabus[18].

20. Voluntary aided schools with a religious character should provide RE in accordance with the trust deed or religious designation of the school, unless parents request the locally agreed syllabus.

21. Foundation schools and voluntary controlled schools with a religious character should follow the locally agreed syllabus, unless parents request RE in accordance with the trust deed or religious designation of the school.

22. RE is also compulsory in faith and non-faith academies as set out in their funding agreements.

6.1.6 Collective worship

23. All maintained schools without a religious character must provide a daily act of broadly Christian collective worship for their pupils. In community schools and non-faith foundation schools, the headteacher is responsible for arranging this after consulting the board. In voluntary aided schools, voluntary controlled schools and foundation schools with a religious character, the board is responsible for arranging collective worship in accordance with the trust deed or religious designation of the school after consulting the headteacher.

24. In some maintained schools without a religious character, the family backgrounds of some or all pupils may lead the headteacher and board to conclude that broadly Christian collective worship is not appropriate. The headteacher can apply to the local SACRE to have the

---

[17] Section 282 of the Companies Act 2006

[18] The locally agreed syllabus is a statutory syllabus of RE prepared under Schedule 31 of the Education Act 1996 and adopted by the LA under that schedule. It must be followed in maintained schools without a designated denomination.

broadly Christian requirement disapplied and replaced by collective worship distinctive of another faith and should consult the board before doing so.

25. Academies without a religious character must also provide a daily act of broadly Christian collective worship by virtue of their funding agreement. An academy wishing to have the broadly Christian requirement disapplied and replaced by collective worship distinctive of another faith should apply to the Secretary of State via the EFA.

6.1.7 Political bias

26. Boards, headteachers and local authorities must not allow the promotion of one-sided political views. This applies both to the teaching of any subject and to extra-curricular activities at the school[19]. Where political issues are covered, opposing views must be presented in a balanced way. The board, headteacher and local authority must also prevent pupils under 12 from taking part in political activities. This covers activities at school or elsewhere. This applies only where a member of staff or anyone acting on behalf of the school or a member of staff arranges the activity.

6.1.8 Disapplication of the national curriculum

27. 'Disapplication' is the decision not to apply elements of the national curriculum in certain circumstances. Where elements of the national curriculum are being disapplied for pupils in individual maintained schools, boards have a role to play in various 'disapplication' processes, depending on the circumstances. Details are in guidance.

6.2 Careers guidance and pupil inspiration

28. Governors have a crucial role to play in connecting their school with the wider community of business and other professional people in order to enhance the education and career aspirations of pupils. This includes helping secure speakers, mentors and work experience placements, all of which can help engage employers in the school and in turn potentially lead to them providing new skilled governors.

29. Maintained schools must secure access to independent careers guidance for pupils in years 8–13. Many academies are subject to the same duty through their funding agreements.

30. Schools must have regard to statutory guidance, which sets a clear framework for the provision of advice and guidance. Academies without the careers requirement are encouraged to follow the guidance as a statement of good practice. It states that boards should:

- ensure that the advice and guidance provided is impartial, includes information on the range of options (including apprenticeships and other vocational pathways) and promotes the best interests of the pupils to whom it is given;
- provide clear advice to the headteacher on which a strategy for advice and guidance can be based that is part of a clear framework linked to outcomes for pupils; and

---

[19] Sections 406 and 407 of the Education Act 1996.

- consider the importance of providing pupils with access to inspiring activities through sustained contacts with employers, mentors and coaches.

31. The board can refer to departmental advice, which sets out some common features of inspirational, high quality advice and guidance.

6.3 The early years foundation stage (EYFS)

32. The EYFS sets out requirements for both learning and development, and safeguarding and welfare provision for children from birth to five. It is mandatory[20] for all providers. This includes maintained schools, academies and all providers on the Early Years Register. The EYFS includes requirements for a number of policies and procedures that may be needed by schools, and boards of establishments delivering the EYFS should reassure themselves that, where such policies and procedures are required, they are in place. Further guidance and supporting materials are available.

6.4 Children with special educational needs (SEN)

33. Legally, a child or young person is defined as having SEN if he or she has a learning difficulty that calls for special educational provision to be made for him or her. A learning difficulty means that the child or young person has significantly greater difficulty in learning than most of their peers, or a disability that prevents or hinders him or her from making use of educational facilities of a kind generally provided for children or young people of the same age in schools within the area of the local authority.

6.4.1 Responsibilities of the board with regard to SEN

34. Boards of maintained schools and academy trusts have legal duties in relation to pupils with SEN.[21]

35. In practice, the functions these duties require of the board can be delegated to a committee, an individual governor or to the headteacher; although the responsibility is still with the board itself to ensure that the functions are carried out. It should decide, with the headteacher, the school's general policy and approach to meeting children and young people's SEN, including those with and without SEN statements or Education, Health and Care (EHC) plans[22]. Statements and EHC plans are documents drawn up by local authorities that set out a child or young person's SEN and the provision that must be made for the child or young person to meet those needs.

36. The board must set up appropriate staffing and funding arrangements and oversee the school's work. The general duties of boards and the 'responsible person' are set out in

---

[20] The EYFS is given legal force through an Order and Regulations made under the Childcare Act 2006.

[21] Part 3 of the Children and Families Act 2014 replaces part 4 of the Education ACT 1996

[22] EHC plans are replacing SEN statements, but the conversion of existing statements will take up to 3 years from September 2014. Existing statements will continue to have force during this time.

paragraphs 1:24 to 1:38 and Chapter 6 of the Special Educational Needs and Disability Code of Practice 0-25 (January 2015).

37. For community, foundation, voluntary schools or maintained nursery schools, the board may also appoint a committee to monitor the school's work for children with SEN.

38. In summary, maintained schools and academy trusts have the following legal duties under the Children and Families Act 2014. Academies must also meet these requirements by virtue of their funding agreement. They must:

- use best endeavours in exercising their functions to ensure that the necessary special education provision is made for any pupil who has SEN;

- ensure that parents or young person are notified by the school when special educational provision is being made for their child, because it is considered that he or she has SEN;

- make sure that the responsible person makes all staff likely to teach the pupil aware of the pupil's SEN;

- make sure that the teachers in the school are aware of the importance of identifying pupils who have SEN and of providing appropriate teaching;

- ensure that there is a qualified teacher designated as special educational needs co-ordinator (SENCO) for the school. A newly appointed SENCO must be a qualified teacher and, where they have not previously been the SENCO at that or any other relevant school for a total period of more than twelve months, they must achieve a National Award in Special Educational Needs Co-ordination within three years of appointment;

- consult the local authority and the boards of other schools when it seems necessary to co-ordinate special educational teaching in the area;

- ensure that pupils with SEN join in the everyday activities of the school together with children without SEN, as far as is compatible with them receiving the necessary special educational provision; the provision of efficient education for all other pupils; and the efficient use of resources;

- take account of the 'SEN and Disability Code of Practice' when carrying out their duties towards all pupils with SEN;

- where a local authority or the First-tier Tribunal (Special Educational Needs and Disability) names a maintained school as the school the child will attend on an SEN statement or Education and Health Care Plan, the board must admit the child to the school. Before naming a maintained school on a statement, the local authority must consult the board of the school (see below);

- cooperate with the local authority in developing the local offer;

- ensure the school produce and publish online its School SEN Information Report in accordance with section 69 of the Children and Families Act 2014; and

- ensure the school has arrangements in place to support children with medical conditions (section 100 Children and Families Act 2014).

39. The responsible person is generally the headteacher, but may be the chair of the board or a governor appointed by the board to take that responsibility. If the responsible person is the headteacher, it is advisable to have one other governor with an interest in SEN.

40. In accordance with the Equality Act 2010, boards are also under a duty to make reasonable adjustments to any provision, criterion or practice to avoid disabled pupils being put at a substantial disadvantage compared to non-disabled pupils. Boards providing auxiliary aids and services is part of the 'reasonable adjustments' duty. Technical guidance on schools' reasonable adjustments duty is available from the Equality and Human Rights Commission.

6.4.2 Admission of pupils with SEN: duties of Admission Authorities (including boards)

41. The 'School Admissions Code'[23] makes clear that all children and young people whose statement of SEN or EHC plan names the school, must be admitted. The admission of pupils with SEN but without statements or EHC plans should be handled in the same way as for all other pupils. If the school is not oversubscribed, all applicants must be offered a place (with the exception of designated grammar schools). Admission authorities must ensure that their arrangements will not disadvantage unfairly, or discriminate against a child with a disability or special educational needs. The 'Admissions Code' applies to all maintained schools in England. Academies must comply, by their funding agreement, with the Code and the law relating to admissions. Further information about school admissions is in Section 10.

6.4.3 Admission of SEN pupils with statements to maintained schools

42. Where the local authority names a maintained school or academy, the board, proprietor or principal of the school is under a duty to admit the child or young person[24].

43. Local authorities are under a duty to consult the board, proprietor or principal of any school or other institution which the authority is considering having named in the statement or EHC plan[25].

44. The general responsibilities of the board in the admission of pupils with SEN to mainstream schools are set out in the School Admissions Code and the Equality Act. They must draw up and implement an 'accessibility plan' for disabled pupils that aims to:

- increase the extent to which disabled pupils can participate in the curriculum;
- improve the physical environment of schools to enable disabled pupils to take better advantage of education, benefits, facilities and services provided; and
- improve the availability of accessible information to disabled pupils.

45. Schools must also take into account the need to provide adequate resources for implementing plans and must regularly review them. An accessibility plan may be a freestanding document but may also be published as part of another document such as the school development plan.

---

[23] The Codes are supported by the School Admissions (Admissions Arrangements and Co-ordination of Admission Arrangements) (England) Regulations 2012, and the School Admissions (Appeal Arrangements) (England) Regulations 2012.

[24] Section 43 of the Children and Families Act 2014.

[25] Section 39 (2) (a) and (6) of the Children and Families Act 2014

SCHOLASTIC

6.4.4 Admission to special schools for pupils with SEN

46. The board of maintained special schools, academy special schools, non-maintained special schools and institutions approved by the Secretary of State to be named in an EHC plan have the same duty to admit as maintained schools (see above). Children or young people without statements or EHC plans can be admitted to special schools in specific circumstances – including for the purposes of assessment or following a change of circumstances[26] (see paragraphs 1.29 and 1.30 of the Special Educational Needs and Disability Code of Practice 0-25, January 2015).

6.4.5 Teachers in maintained schools with responsibility for SEN

47. Boards of maintained schools and academies must ensure that there is a qualified teacher designated as SENCO for the school.[27]

48. The SENCO must be a qualified teacher working at the school. A newly appointed SENCO must be a qualified teacher and, where they have not previously been the SENCO at that or any other relevant school for a total period of more than twelve months, they must achieve a National Award in Special Educational Needs Co-ordination within three years of appointment.

49. The board should reassure itself that the key responsibilities of the SENCO are drawn up and monitor the effectiveness of the way the responsibilities are carried out against a list of illustrative activities, as described in the 'SEN and Disability Code of Practice, 0-25 – January 2015'.

6.5 Looked after children

6.5.1 School admissions

50. Admission authorities are required, with some limited exceptions, to give priority to looked after children, children adopted from care under the Adoption and Children Act 2002 and those who left care under a 'Special Guardianship Order' or 'Residence Order' in their oversubscription criteria[28]. The practical effect of this is that in a school's published admission arrangements, the first and highest oversubscription criterion must be looked after children (see paragraph 1.7 of the Admissions Code). Provisions also apply to schools with a religious character and grammar schools (paragraphs 1.37 and 1.19 of the Admissions Code).

---

[26] Section 33, Children and Families Act 2014

[27] Section 67, Children and Families Act 2014

[28] The School Admissions (School Admissions and Co-ordination of Admission Arrangements) (England) Regulations 2012.

51. The law[29] gives a local authority that looks after a child the right to direct the admission authority of any maintained school to give them a place. This applies, even where the school is currently full, or is in another local authority area (see paragraph 3.19 of the School Admission Code).

52. Boards of all maintained schools are required to appoint a designated teacher to promote the educational achievement of looked after children who are on the school roll[30]. Academies are under an obligation to do this through their funding agreements. Statutory guidance on the roles and responsibilities of designated teachers is available online.

53. Boards must ensure, as a minimum, that:
    ● a designated teacher is appointed;
    ● the teacher undertakes appropriate training;
    ● it considers an annual report from the designated teacher; and
    ● it acts on any issues that the report raises.

54. Regulations specify that the role should be carried out by:
    ● a qualified teacher, within the meaning of section 132 of the Education Act 2002, who has completed the appropriate induction period (if required); or
    ● the headteacher or acting headteacher at the school.

55. All looked after children have a personal education plan (PEP) as part of the care plan that is drawn up by the local authority that looks after them. The PEP forms part of the child's education record[31].

6.6 Assessing attainment and achievement

56. By law, schools must assess pupils' attainment at key points in their compulsory education. These key points are when pupils have completed the early years foundation stage and the programmes of study for key stages 1, 2 and 3, usually at the ages of 5, 7, 11 and 14. There is also a statutory check of phonics at the end of year 1 (age 6). This process is known as statutory assessment.

57. While boards are not directly involved in these processes, they may find the Standards & Testing Agency provide useful background in the context of their responsibilities to drive up school and pupil level performance.

---

[29] Section 97A of the School Standards and Framework Act 1998.

[30] The Children and Young Persons Act 2008, and the Designated Teacher (Looked After Pupils etc.) (England) Regulations 2009.

[31] The Education (Pupil Information) (England) Regulations 2005.

Section 7 – Board Improvement and Inspection

7.1 Self-evaluation

1. Boards should regularly evaluate their own effectiveness. As explained in departmental advice for maintained schools, the chair has a particular responsibility for ensuring the effective functioning of the board. Good chairs also ask for regular feedback from their board to improve their own effectiveness and have an annual conversation with each governor to discuss the impact of their contribution to the work of the board.

2. Academy trusts producing audited accounts for the first time, for example newly converted academies, must set out in the governance statement published within the annual accounts, details of what they have done in their first year to review and develop their governance structure and the composition of the board of trustees. Established trusts should also include in their annual accounts an assessment of the trust's governance, including a review of the composition of the board in terms of skills, effectiveness, leadership and impact. The NGA has launched the NGA Chair of Governors' 360 Appraisal service which provides an analysis of the chair's current performance, and aims to offer comprehensive information regarding areas of strength, as well as areas where improvement may be required (there is a charge for this service).

3. There is a range of tools available that suggest suitable questions to help with self-evaluation. The All-Party Parliamentary Group on Education Governance and Leadership has produced 'Twenty key questions for a board to ask itself' and Twenty-one Questions for Multi-academy Trust Boards. The EEF DIY Evaluation Guide introduces principles of evaluation and provides advice on designing and carrying out small-scale evaluations in schools.

7.2 External Reviews of Governance

4. An objective independent external review of the effectiveness of the board can be a more powerful diagnostic tool. This is particularly important before the board undertakes any significant change – such as conversion to academy status or before a MAT grows significantly. Advice on commissioning and conducting an external review has been published by the NCTL.

5. Where governance is judged by Ofsted to be ineffective, inspectors will include an external review of governance in their recommendations. This will help the school to identify how this aspect of leadership and management may be improved.

6. It is crucial that a board takes this recommendation for an external review as a wake-up call and moves promptly and decisively to commission a high quality independent review and act upon its plan of SMART[32] actions to improve its effectiveness. To inform the focus of the external review, governors should use their attendance at the end of inspection feedback meeting to make sure they understand the reason(s) the external review of governance was recommended and the specific weaknesses inspectors have identified.

---

[32] Specific, measurable, achievable, realistic, timed.

7. It is for the board to decide how the external review will take place, and to commission and pay for it, having regard to the advice published by the NCTL on the form and nature of such reviews. It is essential that boards recognise that an external review of governance should be independent and objective, and not conducted by a "friend" of the board. NCTL, many local authorities, and governor support organisations are able to signpost boards to a growing choice of potential providers that may be commissioned to undertake the review. Such reviews aim to be developmental and do not represent a further inspection.

8. The impact of the external review will be assessed and reported on by inspectors conducting subsequent monitoring visits and the next section 5 inspection. If the board has not undertaken a review by the time of the next section 8 or section 5 inspection, or is not acting on its findings, inspectors may take account of this when evaluating the progress made by the school and the school's overall effectiveness. In some cases, this may lead to a school being judged to be inadequate.

9. The statutory guidance for local authorities on schools causing concern tells local authorities to take note of all recommendations made to maintained schools for an external review. This is because the recommendation could potentially signal that there has been a failure of governance that is prejudicing standards, which could in turn warrant the use of a local authority warning notice to improve.

10. Boards do not need to wait for an Ofsted inspection recommendation to seek a review and can arrange an external review of governance at any time to improve the effectiveness of the work of the board.

7.3 Schools causing concern

11. 'Schools causing concern' refers not just to schools 'eligible for intervention'[33] but also those about which the local authority and/or the Secretary of State have other serious concerns which need to be addressed. This might be where attainment levels are consistently below the floor standards or where the performance is not meeting the expected standards of comparable schools.

12. The statutory guidance, 'Schools Causing Concern – guidance for local authorities' provides information on the legislative requirements for intervening with maintained schools in order to help local authorities fulfil their statutory duty. The guidance specifies that local authorities should not wait for Ofsted to recommend a review of governance to intervene. There is now a new section clearly setting out, in ten key points, what local authorities who champion educational excellence do. This has been added following requests for further clarity on the role of the local authority in school improvement. The guidance will be kept under review and updated as necessary.

13. Local authorities have no statutory powers of intervention with academies. They should contact the Regional Schools Commissioners (RSCs) swiftly where there are concerns about an academy in their area.

---

[33] As defined in Part 4 of the Education and Inspections Act 2006.

7.4 Inspection

14. Ofsted has published the criteria that inspectors will use to judge the effectiveness of a school's governance[34].

15. In every inspection report, inspectors will comment on the quality of governance as part of their overall judgement on the quality of the school's leadership and management. These criteria are consistent with the core functions of all boards set out in Section 1, and take into consideration the board's role in holding the leadership and management of the school to account.

16. These criteria include a strong focus on how boards use data to challenge and hold the headteacher to account, and how they evaluate their own impact and develop their own skills, and will help ensure that good governance gets the praise it deserves. They will also help inspectors identify when a school's governance is not good enough.

17. As part of the inspection process, Ofsted considers responses to its online survey Parent View. The views of parents help inspectors form a picture of how a school is performing and Parent View can provide valuable information on how well the school engages with parents. Governors can access the toolkit Ofsted has developed for schools.

18. The on-site inspection concludes with a final feedback meeting with the school. During this meeting, the lead inspector will ensure that the headteacher and governors are clear about the provisional grades awarded for each key judgement; sufficient detail must be given by the lead inspector to enable all attendees to understand how judgements have been reached and for governors to play a part in beginning to plan how to tackle any areas for improvement. The board should ensure that the chair and as many governors as possible, or appropriate, should be able to attend this meeting.

7.4.1 Section 5 Inspections and Short Inspections

19. Standard school inspections of maintained schools and academies are carried out under section 5 of the Education Act 2005. Details of the inspection process and criteria are set out in Ofsted's Common Inspection Framework, School Inspection Handbook and Inspecting safeguarding in early years education and skills from September 2015.

20. The School Inspection Handbook includes information about the timing of inspections, notification, engagement with governors and the criteria for looking at a board's effectiveness. If governance is assessed to be ineffective, inspectors will recommend an external review of governance.

21. When a school is notified of a section 5 inspection, the governing body must take reasonable steps to notify parents of registered pupils and other prescribed persons[35] of the inspection.

---

[34] The School Inspection Handbook, September 2015.

[35] The Education (School Inspection) (England) Regulations 2005, paragraph 4

22. When it receives the report, the board[36] must arrange for:

- the parents of all pupils to be sent a copy of it within five working days;
- the report to be made available to any member of the public who wishes to see it, at such times and places as may be reasonable; and
- copies of the report to be provided to anyone who asks.

23. Outstanding mainstream schools are exempt from section 5 inspections[37], as are academy converters with a predecessor school judged outstanding at its most recent section 5 inspection[38]. If there are concerns about the performance of an exempt school, Ofsted may inspect the school under section 8 of the Education Act 2005. Such an inspection may be converted into a section 5 inspection if appropriate.

24. Good schools will receive short inspections[39] (a specific type of section 8 inspection) approximately every three years. An Inspector's starting assumption will be that the school remains good, and they will seek evidence to confirm this. If there is sufficient evidence of marked improvement or if the inspector does not obtain sufficient evidence to confirm that the school remains good, the short inspection will be converted into a full section 5 inspection. The decision to convert the inspection to a section 5 inspection does not determine the outcome of that inspection. The School Inspection Handbook – section 8, published by Ofsted, provides information about how Ofsted conducts short inspections. The document also provides information about other types of section 8 inspection, specifically monitoring inspections for schools that require improvement in order to become good or outstanding; monitoring inspections for schools that have serious weaknesses or are subject to special measures; and inspections with no formal designation.

7.4.2 Section 48 inspections

25. The governing body of a voluntary or foundation school or academy that has been designated as having a religious character is responsible for making sure that the content of the school's act of collective worship, and any denominational religious education provided for pupils, is inspected approximately every five years[40] (a 'section 48 inspection'). These aspects of the school's provision will not be included in the section 5 inspection arranged by Ofsted. The governing body may also arrange for the section 48 inspection to cover the spiritual, moral, social and cultural development of pupils at the school. The contractual arrangements for the carrying out of section 48 inspections, including fees, are a matter for the governing body. When choosing an inspector for the section 48 inspection, the governing body (or in the case of a voluntary-controlled school, the foundation governors) must consult one of the following bodies shown in the table below.

---

[36] The Education Act 2005, sections 14 and 16

[37] The Education (Exemption from School Inspection) (England) Regulations 2012

[38] Outstanding nursery schools, special schools and pupil referral units are not exempt from section 5 inspections.

[39] Outstanding schools that are not exempt from section 5 inspections will also receive short inspections. In addition, new schools that have not had a section 5 inspection but have one or more predecessor schools all of which were judged good or better at the most recent section 5 inspection, will receive short inspections.

[40] Section 48 of the Education Act 2005. This applies to academies via clauses in their funding agreement.

School designation	Consultation body
Church of England or Roman Catholic	The appropriate diocesan authority
Jewish	Jewish Studies Education Inspection Service
Methodist	Education Secretary to the Methodist Church
Muslim	Association of Muslim Schools
Sikh	Network of Sikh Organisations
Seventh-day Adventist	Education Department of the British Union Conference of Seventh-day Adventists

Consultation bodies for section 48 inspections

26. A grant is available towards the cost of the section 48 inspection. The process for claiming the grant is managed by the individual faith groups. An inspection report must be prepared within 15 working days of the end of the inspection. Under section 49, the governing body must publish this in the same way as for section 5 inspections.

27. The School Information regulations[41] require boards of maintained schools to publish specified information on a website. This includes publishing details of where and how parents may access the most recent report about the school published by Ofsted, for example, by a link to the school's report on the Ofsted website. The governing body should also consider translating the report into other languages where appropriate.

7.5 Ofsted's involvement in parental complaints about schools

28. By law, and in certain circumstances, Ofsted is able to investigate complaints by parents about their child's school to decide whether to use its inspection powers. It has powers to obtain information to facilitate an investigation. Governors may find it useful to familiarise themselves with Ofsted's guidance to parents.

29. If requested to do so, the governing body must provide Ofsted with any specific information and any other information that the school considers relevant to the investigation of a complaint.

30. Should Ofsted consider it appropriate for the purpose of an investigation that they meet with parents, then the governing body (or in the case of a school which does not have a delegated budget, the local authority) must co-operate with Ofsted in arranging the meeting. This includes allowing a meeting to take place on the school premises, fixing a date for the meeting and notifying parents and the local authority of the meeting. A representative of the governing body and the local authority may also attend the meeting.

31. If Ofsted prepares a report of an investigation, that report must be passed to the governing body (or in the case of a school without a delegated budget, the local authority). The body must then send a copy of the Ofsted report to all registered parents.

---

41 The School Information (England) (Amendment) Regulations 2012.

 **SCHOLASTIC**

Section 8 – Pupil wellbeing

8.1 Promoting the general wellbeing of pupils

1. The Education and Inspections Act 2006 places a duty on boards of maintained schools to promote wellbeing. 'Wellbeing' is defined in the Children Act 2004 as:

    *   physical and mental health and emotional wellbeing;
    *   protection from harm and neglect;
    *   education, training and recreation;
    *   the contribution children make to society; and
    *   social and economic wellbeing.

2. Section 38 of that Act explains the issues around which boards need to consider reassuring themselves that pupils are adequately being cared for and protected from harm while in school.

8.2 Pupil voice

3. The term "pupil voice" refers to ways of listening to the views of pupils and/or involving them in decision-making. The expressions "learner voice" or "consulting pupils" may also be used.

4. The government believes that schools should consider the views of pupils, but it should be up to schools to determine the most effective method to do this.

5. Schools should be aware of the general principles of the United Nations Conventions on the Rights of the Child (UNCRC) – articles 2, 3, 6 and, in particular, article 12 which states the following:

    *   Parties shall assure to the child who is capable of forming his or her own views the right to express those views freely in all matters affecting the child, the views of the child being given due weight in accordance with the age and maturity of the child.
    *   For this purpose, the child, in particular, shall be provided the opportunity to be heard either directly in any judicial and administrative proceedings affecting the child, or through a representative or an appropriate body, in a manner consistent with the procedural rules of national law.

6. The UNCRC has not been incorporated into national law, so there is no statutory duty to comply with it. However, the government has reiterated its commitment to pay 'due regard' to the Convention when new policy is made and legislation proposed. Schools are strongly encouraged to pay due regard to the Convention.

8.3 Behaviour and discipline

7. An academy trust must make sure that a written policy is drawn up and carried out that promotes good behaviour among pupils and defines the sanctions to be adopted where pupils misbehave[42].

8. Maintained school boards must make sure that their school has policies designed to promote good behaviour and discipline among pupils. These policies must include the school's approach to the use of reasonable force to control or restrain pupils. Guidance on reasonable force is in 'Use of Reasonable Force – Advice for headteachers, staff and boards'. Maintained schools should not have a 'no contact' policy.

9. The board must also make, and periodically review, a written statement of principles to help the headteacher determine the measures that make up the school's behaviour policy. This duty cannot be delegated. The board must consult the headteacher, other appropriate members of staff, parents and all registered pupils before making or changing this statement of principles[43]. It must also publish the statement on a website[44]. Information on these responsibilities and statutory guidance to which the board must have regard is given in 'Behaviour and Discipline in Schools: Guidance for Boards' issued by the Secretary of State.

8.3.1 Directing pupils off-site to improve their behaviour

10. The legislation for directing a pupil off-site does not apply to academies. However, an academy may direct a pupil off-site under general powers in their Memorandum and Articles of Association.

11. A maintained school board may send pupils to provision outside school premises that is aimed at improving their behaviour ('directing off-site[45]')[46]. It should make sure that the pupil continues to receive a good education whilst addressing the needs that require intervention. The board may direct a pupil off-site without the parent's consent but should engage with parents, where possible, in the process. There are specific requirements in relation to notifying parents and reviewing the placement.

12. The requirement to review a placement every 30 days was removed in January 2013. A placement may continue beyond the end of the academic year in which it is made. Further information on boards' powers and responsibilities and statutory guidance to which the board must have regard, is provided in 'Alternative Provision: A Guide for Local Authorities, Headteachers and Boards of Schools, Pupil Referral Units and Other Providers of Alternative Provision'.

---

[42] The Education (Independent School Standards) Regulations 2014.

[43] Section 88 of the Education and Inspections Act 2006.

[44] The School Information (England) Regulations 2008 as amended by the School Information (England) (Amendment) Regulations 2012.

[45] This power is routinely delegated to the headteacher.

[46] Section 29A of the Education Act 2002.

8.3.2 Excluding pupils

13. An explanation of boards' legal duties in relation to exclusion, as well as statutory guidance on performing these duties, are provided in 'Exclusion from maintained schools, Academies and pupil referral units in England: A guide for those with legal responsibilities in relation to exclusion'.

14. The board has key responsibilities in relation to reviewing the headteacher's exclusion decisions[47] and must arrange suitable full-time education for excluded pupils from the sixth school day of fixed-period exclusion[48].

15. Academy trusts are also responsible for arranging an independent review panel to consider permanent exclusions, where requested by parents. For maintained schools, this duty rests with the local authority.

16. Boards have a wider role to hold headteachers to account for the lawful use of exclusion. Exclusion must be for disciplinary reasons and all exclusions must be done in line with the legal requirements. Where a pupil is removed from the school premises without being excluded there needs to be a lawful basis for this decision, for example, under the powers of a maintained school to direct a pupil off-site to improve their behaviour (Section 8.3.1).

8.3.3 School attendance

17. The board of a maintained school or academy trust must reassure itself that the school keeps admission and attendance registers in accordance with regulations[49]. Further information and guidance is available in the school attendance section of GOV.UK. The board must make sure that the school provides information requested by the Secretary of State, including the termly absence data the department collects[50].

18. Departmental advice on Children Missing Education is available and all boards must be aware of the statutory requirements placed on them by the statutory guidance Keeping children safe in education.

8.3.4 Parenting measures

19. The maintained school board, academy trust, headteacher and local authority have powers to intervene where a pupil's behaviour or attendance at school becomes problematic[51]. Information on parenting contracts, parenting orders and penalty notices are in section 3 of the statutory guidance 'Advice on school attendance'. Boards, academy trusts, headteachers and local authorities must have regard to it when carrying out their duties.

---

[47] Section 51A of the Education Act 2002 and The School Discipline (Pupil Exclusions and Reviews) (England) Regulations 2012.

[48] Section 100 of the Education and Inspections Act 2006.

[49] Education (Pupil Registration) (England) Regulations 2006.

[50] Section 538 of the Education Act 1996.

[51] Sections 18-23 of the Anti-social Behaviour Act 2003.

8.4 School food and milk

20. Boards must provide paid-for lunches for registered pupils, including nursery pupils who receive education both before and after lunch. This only applies where the parents request them and, in the case of paid-for lunches, where it would not be unreasonable to provide them. These meals must be free for pupils who receive, or whose parents receive, an eligible benefit – the unreasonable clause does not apply to free meals.

21. All state funded schools have a legal duty to provide a free school meal for children in reception, year 1 and year 2. Schools have been provided with substantial funding and support and there is departmental advice available on GOV.UK.

22. Maintained schools and academies that are required to meet the School Food Standards must make lower fat milk or lactose reduced milk available for drinking at least once a day during school hours. Milk must be provided free of charge to pupils eligible for free school meals. Schools may offer milk as many times as they wish, however it must be free to infant and benefits-based free school meal pupils when it is offered as part of their school meal and free to benefits-based free school meal pupils at all other times.[52] Departmental advice on the standards for planning and providing food in schools is available. The advice outlines the requirements to provide food to registered pupils. It also includes information on the School Food Plan, the provision of milk and the free fruit and vegetables scheme.

8.5 School uniform

23. In all schools, boards decide whether there should be a school uniform and other rules relating to pupils' appearance and, if so, what they should be. Departmental advice on school uniform and related policies is available.

8.6 Pupil health and safety

8.6.1 Liability for health and safety

24. The main legislation covering this area is the Health and Safety at Work etc. Act 1974 and regulations made under that Act. The employer is responsible for health and safety.

25. Information about the law on pupil health and safety is in departmental advice on Health and Safety for Schools. This advice summarises health and safety law relevant to schools and explains how it affects boards as well as local authorities, headteachers and other school staff. It covers activities that take place on school premises as well as school trips. The advice applies to all state funded schools. Where the school is the employer, the board must make sure that the school has a policy on health and safety.

---

[52] The Education (Nutritional Standards and Requirements for school Food) (England) Regulations 2007 (SI 2007/2359) as amended by the 2008 regulations (SI 2008/1800) and the 2011 regulations (SI 2011/1190).

8.6.2 Pupils unable to attend school through ill health

26. The duty to provide suitable education for children of compulsory school age who cannot attend school due to illness or injury (alternative provision) rests with local authorities. All schools, including academies, have a key role in ensuring that children on their roll with medical needs also receive a good education. They should involve the relevant local authority immediately when it is clear that a pupil's health will prevent them from attending school for 15 days or more.

8.6.3 Supporting pupils in school with additional health needs

27. Some pupils have additional health needs and may require medicines, adaptations or support to keep well. Boards must oversee the development of policies that cover their own circumstances. Having an additional health needs policy (or including information in health and safety and/or SEN policies) helps ensure consistent arrangements are in place. Where the school is the employer the board will be directly responsible for the policy. For other schools, the local authority will usually delegate the responsibility. The policy should address emergency procedures, training, supervision, record keeping, including storage and disposal. It should also set up a named staff member to coordinate health care needs and to link with parents.

8.6.4 First aid

28. Where they are the employer, boards have overall responsibility for first aid under the Health and Safety (First Aid) Regulations 1981. The regulations set out first aid provision in the work place, and require employers to provide adequate and appropriate equipment, facilities and qualified first aid personnel. It is recommended that schools treat pupils as if they were employees for the purposes of first aid and provide first aid materials and expertise as appropriate, based on a first aid needs assessment. The local authority may delegate this responsibility where it is the employer.

8.6.5 Pupils with disabilities and special educational needs (SEN)

29. The board must reassure itself that the school prepares and implements an accessibility strategy to improve the physical environment of the school for pupils with disabilities and SEN[53]. This should include consideration of particular health and safety needs on the school premises and how these can be met.

30. Boards providing extended services must also consider their duties under the Equality Act 2010. In particular, whether proposed extended services affect their functions and responsibilities towards their pupils, the users of these services or their employees. When services are provided by a third party on schools' premises, either independently of the

---

[53] The Equalities Act 2010

school or on behalf of the school, boards should establish who would be regarded as the service provider with the responsibility to make 'reasonable adjustments' and/or access improvements for disabled users, pupils or employees.

8.6.6 School security

31. In community, voluntary-controlled and community special schools, the responsibility to make the school secure ultimately rests with the local authority as employer. However, it may delegate these duties to the schools. With all other schools, including academies, responsibility rests with the schools.

32. All schools have a common law power to bar troublesome people from the school premises. Boards of foundation, voluntary-aided and foundation special schools also have a power under section 547 of the Education Act 1996 to authorise someone to remove from school premises any intruder causing a disturbance or nuisance. In community and voluntary-controlled schools, the local authority exercises this power unless it is delegated to the school. This power of removal also extends to academies. Departmental advice on this power is on GOV.UK.

33. Schools using automated biometric recognition systems should be aware of their legal duties under the Protection of Freedoms Act 2012. Departmental advice about these duties is on GOV.UK.

8.6.7 Fire Safety

34. Boards of all schools must reassure themselves that annual risk assessments are carried out to make sure that the fire precautions needed in the school are in place.

8.6.8 Playground supervision

35. The number of adults who should be in charge of pupils during lunch and other breaks should be determined locally by the school, having assessed risks and making sure that competent supervisors are available.

8.7 Promoting community cohesion

36. There is a duty for schools to promote community cohesion under the Education and Inspections Act 2006. The board decides how to fulfil this duty in the light of their local circumstances.

8.8 Safeguarding and promoting the welfare of pupils

8.8.1 General duty

37. Section 175 of the Education Act 2002, and regulations under section 157 relating to safeguarding pupils in Independent Schools (including academies), place a duty on the boards of maintained schools, and academy trusts, to have arrangements in place to ensure that they:

    ● carry out their functions with a view to safeguarding and promoting the welfare of children; and

    ● have regard to the statutory guidance issued by the Secretary of State in considering what arrangements they need to make for the purpose of that section.

38. The statutory guidance, Keeping children safe in education, places statutory requirements on all boards. Boards must ensure their schools have effective safeguarding policies and procedures in place that take into account local risks, any statutory guidance issued by the Secretary of State, any local authority guidance and locally agreed inter-agency procedures.

39. Educational settings have a central role to play in the early identification of any welfare concerns about a child, additional needs they might have and indicators of possible abuse, neglect or other safeguarding concerns.

40. To be effective, all schools should work in a multi-agency way with other organisations, share and receive information about individual children in order to protect them from harm. As such all schools should have regard to the guidance set out in Working Together to Safeguard Children 2015.

41. If the school needs further safeguarding advice, advice on designing policies/what to include or safeguarding training they should contact their local safeguarding children's boards. This is in addition to adhering to KCSIE.

8.8.2 Allegations made against staff and volunteers

42. Employers have a duty of care to their employees. Boards should make sure that the school provides effective support for anyone facing an allegation. They must also provide them with a named contact within school if they are suspended. Where an allegation is made, the headteacher or chair of governors should discuss the case with the Designated Officer (DO) immediately. This initial discussion allows both parties to consider the nature, content and context of the allegation and agree an appropriate course of action.

43. Part 4 of Keeping children safe in education sets out the procedures all schools must have in place for dealing with allegations.

44. Schools should ensure that all staff understand, and their procedures make clear, that all allegations should be reported straight away, normally to the headteacher. The procedures should also identify the person, often the chair of governors, to whom reports should be made in the absence of the headteacher, or in cases where the headteacher themselves are

the subject of the allegation or concern. Schools should make available to staff the contact details for the DO responsible for providing advice and monitoring cases.

45. Chairs are expected to work with the headteacher (unless the allegation concerns the headteacher) and DO to confirm the facts about individual cases. They are also expected to reach a joint decision on the way forward in each case. Chairs have a key role in deciding courses of action, including disciplinary action, in those cases where a criminal investigation may not be required. In cases where allegations have been found to be substantiated, the chair should work with the DO and headteacher to determine whether there are any improvements to be made to the school's procedures or practice to help prevent similar events in the future.

46. It is helpful if all board members have training about safeguarding, whether the board acts collectively or an individual member takes the lead. This will make sure they have the knowledge and information needed to perform their functions and understand their responsibilities.

47. Boards should make sure that a senior member of the school's leadership team is designated to take lead responsibility for dealing with safeguarding issues; providing advice and support to other staff; liaising with the local authority; and working with other agencies.

8.8.3 Safe recruitment procedures

48. A key aspect of safeguarding is the vetting of applicants and prospective volunteers working with children to ensure they are not unsuitable. Guidance about these requirements is set out in Section 9.1.3 and in Keeping children safe in education.

49. The statutory guidance 'Disqualification under the Childcare Act 2006' provides information to help schools and local authorities to understand their responsibilities under the Childcare Act 2006 where staff are working in childcare provision in schools.

8.8.4 The Prevent Duty

50. From 1 July 2015 all schools are subject to a duty under section 26 of the Counter-Terrorism and Security Act 2015, in the exercise of their functions, to have "due regard to the need to prevent people from being drawn into terrorism". This duty is known as the Prevent duty. Prevent applies to maintained schools and academies and they must have regard to the Prevent Duty statutory guidance.

51. To accompany the statutory guidance, Departmental advice for schools and childcare providers has been published on preventing children and young people from being drawn into terrorism.

52. If you are concerned that a governor or potential governor may have links to extremism or that a child might be at risk of extremism, or if you have any other concern about extremism in a school please contact our helpline on counter.extremism@education.gsi.gov.uk or 020 7340 7264.

Section 9 – Staffing

1. The main staffing functions of the board in a maintained school, including the appointment, conduct, suspension and dismissal of staff are set out in the School Staffing (England) Regulations 2009[54] and supporting 'Guidance on managing staff employment in schools'.

2. With effect from 1 January 2016 the Secretary of State's powers to issue statutory guidance relating to the appointment, discipline, suspension and dismissal of staff in maintained schools, and the duty on boards and local authorities to have regard to such guidance has been removed. As a result, the guidance is no longer statutory and should be regarded as advice[55].

3. Not all board duties and responsibilities listed in this section fall from the School Staffing Regulations and supporting guidance. Where this is the case, alternative guidance and regulations are given.

4. The requirements on academy trusts are set out in their funding agreements and regulations[56].

5. In addition to their responsibilities under employment law, boards also have responsibilities under the Equality Act 2010. This sets out that employers must not discriminate against employees on any protected grounds (e.g. race or sex) in relation to pay, conditions, opportunities, promotion, training or dismissals. Advice for employers on their responsibilities is available on the ACAS website and further advice to help schools understand how the Equality Act affects them, and how to fulfil their duties under the Act, can be found in departmental advice.

6. The board of a maintained school may delegate all of its functions relating to staff employment in schools[57] with the exception of:

    *   establishing a selection panel to appoint a headteacher or deputy headteacher;

    *   making sure that headteachers benefit from any statutory entitlements and comply with the duties imposed on them which are contained within the STPCD;

    *   responding to any report from the LA that raises serious concerns about the performance of the headteacher;

    *   establishing procedures for the regulation of conduct and discipline of staff, and making sure that safer recruitment procedures are applied.

7. Although the responsibility is still with the board to ensure any delegated functions are carried out.

8. Academy trusts are free to decide which functions they delegate.

---

[54] The School Staffing (England) Regulations 2009 are amended by The School Staffing (England) (Amendment) Regulations 2012 and The School Staffing (England) (Amendment) Regulations 2014.

[55] Cabinet Office Deregulation Act 2015 in respect sections 35(8) and 36(8) of the Education Act 2002.

[56] The Education (Independent School Standards) Regulations 2014.

[57] Regulation 4 of the School Staffing (England) Regulations 2009.

9.1 Appointing staff

9.1.1 Appointing a headteacher

9. Appointing a headteacher is a pivotal decision in the life of a school. It is crucial that a board has the skills it needs to carry out a thorough and effective selection process. Governors may need to seek help or training, for example, on good interviewing techniques or on how to secure meaningful and accurate references.

10. 'A guide to selecting and recruiting a new headteacher', developed jointly with the NGA, is available on the NCTL website.

11. Every maintained school must have a headteacher[58]. The board must notify the local authority in writing of any headteacher vacancy, advertise the post in a manner considered appropriate, and appoint a selection panel. The board must appoint a member of staff to carry out the functions of a headteacher pending the appointment of a headteacher or in the absence of a headteacher.

12. The Education (Independent School Standards) Regulations 2014 require an academy to publish the name of a headteacher.

13. As part of the appointment process the board of a maintained school or academy trust may ask for details about whether a headteacher or teacher at the school has been subject to capability procedures in the previous two years. A maintained school must provide this. The trust of any academy that opened after April 2013 must also provide this information[59].

14. Where the local authority is the employer[60], a representative of the authority may attend proceedings relating to the selection or dismissal of any teacher. The board must consider any advice offered by the representative. Where the board is the employer[61] and where it has been agreed the local authority has advisory rights, the board must consider any advice offered.

9.1.2 Discrimination in appointments and during service

15. Employers must be aware of their responsibilities in respect of discrimination within equalities legislation[62] when recruiting staff and throughout the employment relationship.

16. Employers are not allowed to ask about the health and disability of any candidate until after a job offer has been made, unless such an enquiry is to establish their capability to carry out a function intrinsic to the work concerned. Boards and academy trusts must make 'reasonable adjustments' to their employment arrangements, practices or premises if such changes would

---

[58] Sections 35(3) and 36(3) Education Act 2002.

[59] Subject to the terms of its funding agreement an academy that opens earlier than April 2013 may also be required to provide information relating to a teacher's capability procedures.

[60] Community, voluntary-controlled, community special or maintained nursery schools (section 35 of the Education Act 2002).

[61] Foundation, voluntary-aided and foundation special schools (section 36 of the Education Act 2002)

[62] The Equality Act 2010.

help alleviate any disadvantage suffered by a disabled employee compared to a non-disabled person.

17. Legislation[63] sets out the circumstances in which maintained schools, designated by the Secretary of State as having a religious character, have some discretion to take into account certain religious or denominational considerations in making specified employment decisions relating to their staff (i.e. decisions on appointment, remuneration, promotion and dismissal). Guidance on the subject is provided in Chapter 9 of the department's 'Guidance on managing staff employment in schools', entitled 'Staff at schools with a religious character'.

18. In relation to academies, converters follow the position of the school prior to conversion. New academies with a religious character are able to appoint all their teaching staff based on faith in line with their designation, and can appoint support staff by application of religious criteria, where they can demonstrate a genuine occupational requirement for doing so.

9.1.3 Employment checks

19. Specific and detailed information about required safer recruitment practices can be found within 'Keeping children safe in education'. Those governors responsible for appointing staff in schools should make themselves familiar with Part 3: Safer recruitment.

20. Once the board or academy trust has chosen a preferred candidate, and before any appointment is made, it must:

    - check the identity of the candidate;
    - their right to work in the United Kingdom[64] and whether the candidate has the necessary health and mental fitness to teach[65];
    - whether any reasonable adjustments are required to allow teaching staff to provide effective and efficient teaching; and
    - when appointing into teaching positions that the individual concerned is not prohibited from carrying out such work.

21. For the majority of work in schools, boards and academy trusts must obtain, for all new appointments, an enhanced Disclosure and Barring Service (DBS) certificate before, or as soon as practicable after appointment. If the work is within the scope of 'regulated activity' relating to children[66], the enhanced certificate will need to include information to confirm the person is not barred from working with children (barred list information). Where the person will begin work before the DBS certificate is available a separate barred list check must be obtained before work commences.

---

[63] Sections 58 to 60 of the School Standards and Framework Act 1998.

[64] Regulations 12 and 24 of the School Staffing (England) Regulations 2009 for maintained schools and for academy schools and AP academies, in line with the requirements set out in their funding agreement.

[65] The Education (Health Standards) (England) Regulations 2003.

[66] As defined in Part 1 of Schedule 4 to the Safeguarding Vulnerable Groups Act 2006.

22. Boards will usually make the request for the DBS certificates/checks through their LA, which acts as an umbrella body for the DBS; academy trusts will have their own umbrella body arrangements. Further guidance on these checks is available on the DBS website and within 'Keeping children safe in education'.

23. Where the applicant has lived outside the UK, the board must carry out additional checks to determine the person's suitability. An overseas criminal record check or a certificate of good conduct from the relevant embassy or police force should be obtained where possible. Advice on the criminal records information that can be obtained from overseas police forces can be found on GOV.UK.

24. Employers have a duty[67] to check potential employees' documents before employing them, to ensure they have the right to work in the UK. Further guidance on the checks needed to establish the right to work in the UK is available on GOV.UK

25. Boards should also:

- request written information about previous employment history, which should be scrutinised for inconsistencies, contradictions, or incomplete information;

- source references, both written and via telephone, directly from the applicant's current or former employer for all short-listed candidates, including internal ones, before interview, so that any issues of concern they may raise can be explored further with the referee, and taken up with the candidate at interview. Boards should not rely on open, 'to whom it may concern', references;

- consider asking the candidate's current employer for details of any capability history in the previous two years, and the reasons for this.

26. When sharing information employers should make sure that they act in accordance with the Data Protection Act 1998 and data protection principles, making sure that the information is provided fairly and lawfully to prospective employers.

27. The board or academy trust must reassure itself that all appropriate suitability checks have been undertaken and that the school keeps a single central record, detailing the range of checks it has carried out on its staff.

9.1.4 The Employer Access Online system

28. When making appointments, boards will need to reassure themselves that mechanisms are in place within the school to check that any person employed to teach has the required teaching qualifications, has successfully completed any statutory induction required and is not prohibited by the Secretary of State from carrying out teaching work. The NCTL's Employer Access Online system, which is accessed via the Department's Secure Access portal, can be used to confirm teaching qualifications, the satisfactory completion of the necessary induction period for UK trained teachers and to check that a prohibition order has not been imposed on the individual.

---

[67] The School Staffing (England) Regulations 2009 and The Education (Independent School Standards) Regulations 2014.

9.2 Statutory induction for newly qualified teachers (NQTs)

29. The board or academy trust must be satisfied that the institution in which the induction of NQTs is being served has the capacity to support the NQT and that the headteacher is fulfilling their responsibilities. In addition, charges by appropriate bodies for their services, in respect of induction in maintained schools, will be directed to the board. The full statutory guidance is on GOV.UK.

9.3 Teacher qualifications

30. The board of a maintained school or non-maintained special school should be aware that teachers must hold qualified teacher status (QTS)[68] (unless the teacher satisfies one of the requirements or conditions specified in the Schedule to the appropriate regulations). This also applies to academy trusts whose funding agreement states that any teachers that it employs must hold QTS.

31. Teachers who hold Qualified Teacher Learning and Skills (QTLS) status and membership of the Education and Training Foundation (ETF), will automatically be recognised as qualified teachers in schools in England, and do not need QTS. They will also be exempt from serving a statutory induction period in schools. This will allow them to be appointed to permanent posts in maintained schools in England and they will be paid on the qualified teachers' pay scale. They will continue to be recognised as qualified teachers providing they remain a member of the ETF.

32. The same statutory requirement to hold QTS is not in place for teachers employed by academies unless the academy's funding agreement retains a clause to that effect. An academy may be required through its funding agreement to employ teachers with QTS, but the department may agree to relax this requirement if requested by an academy. Even in academies, special educational needs coordinators and designated teachers for looked after children must have QTS. All teachers in special academies must hold QTS. There is no requirement for teaching staff in free schools to hold QTS.

33. The Specified Work Regulations allow maintained schools to employ industry experts as instructors to teach, where specialist qualifications and/or experience are required, as a first choice and on a permanent basis. Instructors will continue to be classed as unqualified teachers and will be paid at the appropriate level of the unqualified teachers' pay scale (in maintained schools).

---

[68] Regulation 3(1) of the Education (Specified Work) (England) Regulations 2012.

◾SCHOLASTIC

9.4 Teacher and headteacher appraisal

34. Academies are free to determine their own appraisal process and may adopt the requirements for maintained schools if they wish.

35. Boards in maintained schools have a statutory duty[69] to:

- appoint an external adviser for advice and support on the headteacher's appraisal and to consult that adviser on setting objectives for, and appraisal of, the headteacher;
- inform the headteacher of the standards against which their performance will be assessed;
- set objectives for the headteacher;
- appraise the performance of the headteacher, assessing their performance of their role and responsibilities against the relevant standards and their objectives;
- assess the headteacher's professional development needs and action needed to address them;
- make a recommendation on headteacher's pay, where relevant;
- give the headteacher a written report of their appraisal which includes the assessments and recommendation above;
- determine the appraisal period that applies to teachers (including headteachers)[70];
- adopt a document that sets out the appraisal process for teachers (including headteachers) and make that document available to teachers; and
- make sure that headteachers carry out their duties in respect of appraising other teachers (including recommendations on pay).

36. In practice, boards will want, in relation to the appraisal of the headteacher, to:

- satisfy themselves that the external advisor has the skills, experience and objectivity to provide them with advice and support;
- consider whether to delegate the headteacher's appraisal to a sub-group;
- satisfy themselves that the headteacher's objectives are SMART[71];
- decide which standards they will use to assess the headteacher's performance. They must assess headteachers' performance against the Teachers' Standards and may also wish to use the National Standards for headteachers;
- decide what arrangements to make for observing the headteacher's performance, including any arrangements for classroom observation where headteachers teach; and
- satisfy themselves that appraisal evidence informs other decisions, for example, on professional development and pay.

---

[69] The Education (School Teachers' Appraisal) (England) Regulations 2012.

[70] Regulation 5 of The Education (School Teachers' Appraisal) (England) Regulations 2012.

[71] Specific, measurable, achievable, realistic, timed.

37. In relation to appraisal more widely, boards will want to:

- scrutinise the content of the school's draft appraisal policy carefully to make sure that it will support effective appraisal in the school, challenging the headteacher as appropriate. In particular they will want to satisfy themselves with:

- the provision that is made for the appraisal of teacher performance against the Teachers' Standards and their objectives;

- the arrangements being made for classroom observation, now that there is no annual limit on the amount of observation that can take place;

- any arrangements for the headteacher to delegate the duty of managing the performance of teachers to others.

- satisfy themselves that the appraisal policy is being implemented effectively and fairly in the school, challenging the headteacher on how objectives and assessments are quality assured and moderated;

- satisfy themselves that appraisal evidence informs other decisions for example, on professional development and pay; and

- keep the policy under review and amend it as necessary.

9.5 Pay and conditions of service

38. The department has published advice to help boards to determine their approach to teachers' pay.

39. The relevant body (usually the board) must adopt and take full responsibility for maintaining, updating and implementing a robust and considered pay policy that:

- sets out clearly the basis on which all decisions that determine pay will be made and communicated to all teachers;

- sets out the extent to which specific functions relating to pay determination will be delegated to others, such as the headteacher;

- explains the role that the relevant body will play in determining decisions relating to individual teachers;

- fully complies with all relevant aspects of equalities legislation;

- sets the date by which it will determine teachers' annual pay review; and

- establishes procedures for addressing teachers' grievances, in relation to their pay, in accordance with the ACAS Code of Practice.

40. Such a policy must conform to any statutory provisions that are set out within the STPCD. Boards must assure themselves that the arrangements proposed for linking appraisal to pay progression are robust and can be applied consistently.

41. All teachers in maintained schools are subject to statutory conditions relating to their professional duties and working time[72]. In addition to these statutory conditions, teachers are subject to other conditions of employment laid down in their contracts of employment, such as those that provide for sick pay and maternity leave. The terms of certain local agreements may also be incorporated into their contracts of employment.

42. In schools where the local authority is the legal employer, the pay and conditions of service for school support staff must be on the scale of grades determined by the local authority. In foundation and voluntary-aided schools, the board is free to determine the pay and conditions of support staff.

43. Academy trusts are free to set their own pay and conditions of service for any teachers and support staff[73].

9.6 Discipline, grievance and capability procedures

44. The board of maintained schools must approve disciplinary and grievance procedures for staff. Academy trusts may delegate this duty. Maintained school boards must also approve capability procedures for dealing with staff underperformance and provide a procedure to enable staff to appeal against a decision to dismiss them. Boards may adopt the department's 'Model capability policy for teachers'.

45. Advice for boards about establishing these procedures is provided in 'Guidance on managing staff employment in schools'. Boards should be mindful of their obligations under employment law and take into account the 'Advisory, Conciliation and Arbitration Service (ACAS) Code of Practice'.

46. Academy trusts are responsible for establishing their own staff procedures and need to take account of the relevant law and guidance.

9.7 Referring cases to the NCTL and Disclosure and Barring Service

47. The Education Act 2011 gave the Secretary of State for Education responsibility for the regulation of the teaching profession from 1 April 2012. The NCTL operate the arrangements on behalf of the Secretary of State for Education. Guidance on Teacher misconduct: regulating the teaching profession is available.

48. The regulatory arrangements cover teachers in all schools in England and only deal with cases of serious misconduct. Less serious cases of misconduct, and all cases of incompetence, should be dealt with at a local level. Employers, including an employment or supply agency, must consider whether to refer a teacher who has been dismissed for serious misconduct, or would have been dismissed had they not resigned.

---

[72] Part 7 of the STPCD.

[73] Where a maintained school converts to an academy, at the point of transfer the existing terms and conditions of teachers and support staff are protected under The Transfer of Undertakings (Protection of Employment) Regulations 2006 (TUPE) arrangements. The STPCD will, therefore, remain relevant to any teachers whose contract has not been renegotiated.

49. Members of the public, other regulators and the police are also able to refer cases of misconduct. The NCTL's Employer Access system holds a list of teachers who have been prohibited from working in schools in England.

50. Employers must refer to the DBS anyone who has harmed or poses a risk of harm to a child and who has been removed from working (paid or unpaid) in regulated activity, or would have been removed had they not left. The DBS will consider whether to bar the person. Referrals should be made as soon as possible after the resignation or removal of the individual. Guidance on referrals is provided by the DBS.

9.8 Trade unions and disputes with staff

51. Employers are bound to recognise those trades unions with which they have a voluntary recognition agreement or which they are required to recognise by the Central Arbitration Committee. In foundation and voluntary-aided schools, the board as employer will recognise such unions; for academy schools it will be the trust; and for community and voluntary-controlled schools it will be the local authority.

52. Trade union recognition and the continuation of consultation and bargaining rights are protected under the Transfer of Undertakings (Protection of Employment) Regulations (TUPE) (2006). This means that for staff transferring from an existing school to an academy trust, any trade union recognition agreements applying to transferring staff will also transfer, as will any collective agreements in force at the time of transfer. The process for trade union recognition is set out in the Trade Union and Labour Relations (Consolidation) Act 1992 (TULR(C)A). Further information about ACAS and the advice it provides on trade union recognition is on the ACAS website.

53. Further advice on handling strike action in schools can be found on GOV.UK.

9.8.1 Employment tribunals

54. Employment tribunals hear complaints lodged against employers on the grounds that they have discriminated against individuals or failed to respect their rights under employment law. Tribunals can order an employee to be re-engaged or reinstated, and they can award compensation. Guidance on the role of employment tribunals is on the GOV.UK and ACAS websites.

9.9 Teachers' Pension Scheme (TPS)

55. The TPS is an occupational, public service pension scheme for teachers governed by regulations[74]. The department have overall responsibility for the TPS whilst the day-to-day administration is undertaken by Capita Teachers' Pensions.

---

[74] The Teachers' Pensions Regulations 2010 and The Teachers' Pension Scheme Regulations 2014.

56. On 1 April 2015, the TPS changed for most members. Full information regarding the changes to the TPS and the level and range of benefits available, including advice on ill health retirement and retired teachers and re-employment, is on the TP website, which presents information from the perspective of both the member and the employer. Employers have a crucial role in the successful administration of the TPS. Details of the full range of employer duties are on the TP Employer Hub.

9.10 The Local Government Pension Scheme

57. An academy trust that has entered into academy arrangements is a Scheme employer in the Local Government Pension Scheme (LGPS) and is listed in paragraph 20 of Part 1 of Schedule 2 to the LGPS (Administration) Regulations 2013. This means that the non-teaching staff employed by academy trusts are automatically eligible for membership of the LGPS and existing members in a maintained school retain eligibility when a school becomes an academy. The change in legal status, when a former maintained school is replaced by an academy, means that the academy trust becomes an LGPS employing authority in its own right. Academy trusts, free schools, studio schools and UTCs are also LGPS employers.

Section 10 – Admissions and organisational changes

10.1 School admissions

1. The purpose of the School Admissions Code is to ensure that all school places for maintained schools (excluding maintained special schools[75]) and Academies are allocated and offered in an open and fair way. The Code has the force of law, and where the words 'must' or 'must not' are used, these represent a mandatory requirement.

2. The School Admissions Code is the statutory guidance that schools must follow when carrying out duties relating to school admissions. This handbook is a summary reference but is not a substitute for the full Codes.

3. The Code applies to admissions to all maintained schools in England, and academies (including free schools, studio schools and UTCs) are required by their funding agreements to comply with the Code and the law relating to admissions. The Code should be read alongside the School Admission Appeals Code and other guidance and law that affect admissions and admission appeals in England.

4. Boards, local authorities, Schools Adjudicators and admission appeal panels (see below) must act in accordance with the Codes.

5. 'Admission authorities' are responsible for setting fair and transparent admission arrangements; making admission decisions and arranging admission appeals in accordance with the Codes. Admission authorities decide which children are admitted by applying the admissions criteria they have set and published. For community and VC schools, the local authority is the admission authority; for all other schools it is the board or academy trust[76]. Governors of VA schools, foundation schools or academies, therefore, should understand their roles and responsibilities in relation to admissions.

10.1.1 Admissions arrangements

6. Admission authorities must set admission arrangements annually, notify their local authority and publish the arrangements on their website in accordance with the School Admissions Code. When changes to the admission arrangements are proposed, admission authorities must consult. Consultation must last at least eight weeks between 1 November and 1 March so that the arrangements are finalised by 15 April. There should be a clear decision by the board to determine (agree as final) a set of arrangements by 15 April, even where the arrangements have not changed from the previous year. Local authorities must publish on their website by 1 May, details of where the set arrangements for all schools can be found. From September 2015, new dates and timings for consultation, determination and publication will apply. These are set out in the Code.

---

[75] A maintained special school is a school maintained by the local authority, specially designed to make special educational provision for pupils with special educational needs.

[76] A local authority can delegate admissions to the governing bodies of community and voluntary-controlled schools.

7. Admission authorities for schools with a sixth form must ensure they have determined and published admission arrangements for entry into the sixth form, if they intend to admit external applicants.

8. Admission authorities must, as part of setting their admission arrangements, set a clear published admission number (PAN), which states the number of applicants they will admit where enough applications are received. A board of a community or VC school can object to the Adjudicator if they disagree with their PAN (which will be set by the local authority as admission authority).

9. Admission authorities cannot refuse a child a place if the school is undersubscribed (fewer applications than the PAN). The only exception is where the child has been permanently excluded from two or more schools within the past two years or, in the case of selective schools, where the child has not met the required academic standard. Regardless of faith, a child must be offered a place in a school with a religious designation if they apply to the school and it is undersubscribed.

10. Admission authorities cannot introduce new arrangements to select all or part of their intake based on high academic ability.

11. The infant class size limit is 30 pupils per teacher. Additional children may be admitted under limited exceptional circumstances, which are set out in the Code.

12. Admission authorities for oversubscribed schools must keep a waiting list for at least the first term in the normal year(s) of admission. They must order the waiting list and give priority for places solely according to their published oversubscription criteria, regardless of when an application was made or how long the child's name has been on the list.

13. A place in a nursery class does not guarantee admission to the reception class. Parents must make a separate application for any transfer from nursery to primary school.

14. Any person or body can make an objection to the Schools Adjudicator about the admission arrangements of any state-funded school. The objection must be made by 30 June in the year in which the admission arrangements are determined. Further information on how to make an objection is available on the Office of the Schools Adjudicator website.

10.1.2 Admission appeals

15. Admissions appeal panels are independent panels set up by admissions authorities in line with the School Admission Appeals Code. They hear appeals against admission decisions. The Appeals Code provides details on appeal procedures and outlines a parent's or child's right of appeal. Where a panel finds in favour of the parent or child, the decision is binding on the school.

16. Free training packs for appeal panel members are available at Information for School and College Governors (ISCG), Avondale Park School, Sirdar Road, London W11 4EE.

17. Further information is available on the ISCG website.

10.2 The school day and school year

18. Academies set their own school day and term dates. The provisions on school sessions do not apply to them. The board will decide the length of the school day, including session times and breaks, taking into account the recommendation of the headteacher. School employers determine the term dates[77]. Maintained schools must open for at least 380 sessions (190 days) in a school year[78]. The school year must begin after July. If a school is prevented from meeting and it is not reasonably practicable for arrangements to be made for it to make up the lost session(s), it can be deemed to have been open for the required 380 sessions.

10.3 Conversion to academy status

19. Boards play a pivotal role in deciding whether conversion to academy status is right for their school. The board must pass a resolution confirming its desire to convert to academy status before the school can make a formal application to start the conversion process. Those who appoint any foundation governors must also give their consent before the board can apply.

20. Maintained school boards considering conversion to academy status must consult people that they think appropriate. Schools with a religious designation must also consult their Diocesan Board or relevant religious authority and must secure that body's consent before submitting an application.

21. Schools can consult in a number of ways such as via a website, newsletters and face-to-face meetings or discussions. It is important that people being consulted are given all relevant information about what is proposed and have a fair chance to respond. There is no set time for carrying out the consultation, although it is useful to have discussions early in the process. The consultation process must be completed before a funding agreement is signed with the Secretary of State.

22. The board must be able to confirm that a consultation has taken place, when it was carried out and that the views obtained were properly considered. Schools do not have to provide documentary evidence of this as part of the academy conversion process but will need to make sure it is available on request.

23. Under equalities legislation, public bodies must have 'due regard' to the need to eliminate discrimination, promote equality of opportunity and foster good relations when carrying out their duties. Boards should consider whether they have met the requirements under the Equality Act 2010 or whether any further action needs to be taken in relation to their conversion to academy status.

---

[77] Section 32 of the Education Act 2002.

[78] Education (School Day and School Year) (England) Regulations 1999.

24. When a school converts to an academy, TUPE legislation entitles staff to transfer under the same employment terms and conditions. The current employer (the local authority in community and voluntary-controlled (VC) schools and the board in foundation and voluntary-aided schools) has a statutory obligation to inform their employees' representatives (i.e. trade union or elected representatives) that:

    - the transfer is to take place;
    - the date of the transfer and the reasons for it;
    - the legal economic and social implications of the transfer; and
    - whether the current employer, or as the new employer, the academy trust, expects to make changes connected to the transfer that will affect the employees' terms and conditions of employment and, if so, what those changes will be.

25. It is also good practice to provide this information to the employees themselves at an early stage in the process. Employers should consider seeking legal advice to make sure that they can identify the potential implications for employees of the transfer.

26. Where an employer (current or new) decides that changes are to be made to employees' terms and conditions of employment, it is important to make sure that the process for introducing those changes complies with employment law. This will usually involve consultation both with employees' representatives and with the affected employees.

27. A collection of documents that schools converting to an academy will need as they go through the conversion process is available on GOV.UK. The NCTL's 'Academies online resource' will help schools considering a move to academy status. Free membership is required to access the resource.

28. The Education Funding Agency has published Top Tips for governors of schools on the path to becoming an academy.

10.3.1 Support for another school

29. Schools which convert to academy status should work to support one or more other schools, whether maintained schools or academies. Academies can choose what they do to support another school or schools and how they do it, but it must be intended to raise standards. This is a key aspect of the creation of a self-improving school system. The board of an academy has a role in making sure that it delivers its commitment to other schools, however it is done. The board might itself be directly involved in offering support to raise standards of school governance. To keep bureaucracy to a minimum this commitment will not be regularly monitored by the department.

10.4 Other organisational changes

30. School type determines the 'prescribed alterations' and significant changes that the board can propose. Examples are:

- a change of school type;
- transfer of site or discontinuance of a split site;
- co-educational to single sex or vice versa;
- changes to SEN etc.; or
- school closure (including in order to add, change or remove religious character).

31. Boards are able to make some changes to their school's size and characteristics without following a statutory process, such as:

- a change of age range of up to 2 years (provided that this does not add a sixth form);
- expanding the school;
- adding boarding provision.

32. Local authorities will still be able to propose these changes, but will need to follow a statutory process to do so. Information on the roles and processes to be followed[79] are available.

33. Academy trusts can apply to the Secretary of State, via the Education Funding Agency (EFA) to make changes to their existing arrangements.

34. Fast track significant changes – expansions, age range changes (by up to three years), adding boarding provision and amending admissions arrangements in old style funding agreements – do not require a formal business case. Approval from the Secretary of State is still required but the majority of these requests will be approved, provided that adequate local consultation has taken place, financial arrangements are sound, and that appropriate planning permissions have been secured. Guidance on these changes is available on GOV.UK.

10.4.1 Closure of a voluntary or foundation school

35. In addition to the method above, the board of a foundation, VA or VC school may close their school by giving two years' notice. This must follow the process set out in section 30 of the School Standards and Framework Act 1998.

10.4.2 Board as decision maker

36. The board of a maintained school (with the exception of maintained nursery school) is the decision maker for 'foundation' proposals[80] unless referred to the schools' adjudicator by the local authority in 'prescribed' circumstances[81].

---

[79] The Education and Inspections Act 2006, the School Organisation (Establishment and Discontinuance of Schools) (England) Regulations 2013, the School Organisation (Prescribed Alterations to Maintained Schools) (England) Regulations 2013, and the School Organisation (Removal of Foundation, Reduction in Number of Foundation Governors and Ability of Foundation to Pay Debts) (England) Regulations 2007.

[80] A change of category to foundation; the acquisition of a Trust or acquisition of a foundation majority

[81] Schedule 1, paragraph 10 of The School Organisation (Prescribed Alterations to Maintained Schools) (England) Regulations 2007, as amended.

37. Following a VA school board decision, in 'prescribed' circumstances, the local authority, Roman Catholic and/or Church of England diocese, or the EFA, may request referral to the schools' adjudicator. The request must be made within four weeks of the board decision. The board must submit the proposals, and any objections or comments relating to them, to the adjudicator within one week of receiving the request.

10.4.3 Right of appeal by a board

38. The board of a foundation, foundation special, voluntary controlled or voluntary aided school can appeal to the schools' adjudicator if they disagree with the local authorities' decision on any 'prescribed alteration' or closure proposals for its school. Any request for referral must be made within four weeks of the local authorities' decision.

10.4.4 Revocation of proposals

39. Where statutory proposals are approved, the proposer must carry them out. If, however, circumstances change significantly and it is difficult or no longer appropriate to carry out approved proposals, the original proposer can publish 'revocation proposals'. Approval of the revocation proposals removes the duty to carry out the original proposals.

40. Where the board of a foundation or voluntary school with a religious character publishes foundation 'revocation proposals', it must notify the local Roman Catholic and/or Church of England diocese, the EFA (where appropriate) and any trustees, of its decision.

10.4.5 Removal of a trust or reduction in the number of foundation governors

41. The board of a foundation school may remove the Trust or alter the school's instrument of government so that the Trust no longer appoints the majority of governors. This would apply where they believe it to be in the best interests of the school. It applies only to Trust schools that have been established, or have acquired their Trust, under the Education and Inspections Act 2006. This is a statutory process[82]. When a Trust is removed, the school becomes a foundation school without a foundation.

---

[82] The School Organisation (Removal of Foundation, Reduction in Number of Foundation Governors and Ability of Foundations to Pay Debts) (England) Regulations 2007.

Section 11 – Control and community use of school premises

11.1 Day-to-day control of school premises

1. Academy trusts are responsible for the day-to-day running of the school land and buildings and health and safety of the pupils. Guidance on when consent to dispose of or acquire land and grant to take on leases and joint use agreements is set out in the Academies Financial Handbook and in more detail in the Academy property transactions: advice and forms.

2. All maintained school boards control the occupation and use of premises during and outside school hours. This means that boards have control over what happens in school buildings and grounds. They are also responsible for deciding how school facilities are used. There are limited exceptions to this, such as:

   ● in a school where a trust deed transfers control to someone other than the board;

   ● where a Transfer of Control Agreement (TofCA) has been made (see below);

   ● where the local authority issues directions[83] on how school premises should be used, e.g. regular booking for youth or community groups; or

   ● where the school is needed for local or general elections.

11.2 Use of premises for extended activities and community services

3. Schools can accommodate extended and community services. Examples include after-school clubs, adult education, out-of-school childcare (including breakfast clubs and holiday care), and sport and youth clubs. Some schools offer or rent out their facilities to voluntary organisations. Joint use good practice principles on structuring these arrangements are included in the Academy property transactions: advice and forms.

4. These arrangements can benefit schools, their pupils and parents, and their local communities. Schools offering extended services may benefit from improved behaviour and attendance. These arrangements can also enable schools to make the best use of their facilities, which may otherwise be underused before and after the school day and in school holidays.

5. Boards may not use their delegated budget shares for anything other than the purposes of the school. The term 'purposes of the school' would normally be interpreted as including all activities that bring an educational benefit to pupils at the school. The term also includes spending on pupils registered at other maintained schools and providing community facilities for charitable services[84].

---

[83] Directions should be reasonable and not interfere too much with the board's control. For example, the local authority should not require premises to be made available to it if this would mean the board breaking a booking agreement.

[84] See section 27 of the Education Act 2002.

6. Boards can charge for the provision of extended and community services[85].

7. An academy trust's articles of association set out the powers that the trust may exercise in pursuit of its charitable object. The current model articles allow the academy trust 'to provide educational facilities and services to students of all ages and the wider community for the public benefit'.

8. Academies should also consult their funding agreement. The current model funding agreement says that the academy 'will be at the heart of its community, promoting community cohesion and sharing facilities with other schools and the wider community'. The funding agreement will set out how the grant available from the Secretary of State can be used.

11.3 Transfer of control agreements

9. Boards can enter into a Transfer of Control Agreement (TofCA) as a way of sharing control of the school premises with another body, or transferring control to it. The other body, known as the 'controlling body', will continue to occupy and use the premises during the times specified in the agreement. Transferring control of the premises to local community groups, sports associations and service providers can allow school facilities to be used without needing ongoing management or administrative time from the school staff. The board of a community school must obtain the local authority's consent before entering into a TofCA that transfers control during school hours.

10. It may not be necessary for a school to enter into a TofCA to enable another organisation to use their premises. Alternative options for a school include retaining overall control of the premises while subletting use of part of their premises to another organisation or entering into a Service Level Agreement with another organisation.

11.4 Provision of childcare and other community services

11. Many schools and academies offer comprehensive programmes of before and after school and holiday care, and other activities, throughout the year. These programmes support pupils and parents, place the schools and academies at the hearts of their communities, and can generate profit that can be reinvested to improve services.

12. There are three possible arrangements that would allow an academy to operate a nursery on their premises:

    *   direct provision of a nursery by the academy trust as a charitable activity within the academy's objects;

    *   provision of a nursery through a wholly-owned subsidiary company of the academy trust;

    *   the academy trust contracts out nursery provision to an independent provider (which may or may not be a charity; and in which a trustee may have an interest).

---

[85] See section 27(3) of the Education Act 2002.

13. In deciding what, if any, extended activities to offer and in making decisions on the form any such activities should take, boards should:

- make sure that extended activities or services benefit the public (or in an academy's case, comply with its charitable objects) and that any profits made are reinvested in the service or in the school;

- make sure extended activities or services do not conflict with their statutory duties, in particular their duty to promote high educational achievement in the school;

- make sure that any childcare for children provided by the school and any other childcare provided is registered where necessary or appropriate with Ofsted.

14. Maintained schools may change the age range of their school to set up early years provision (in which case the children would be pupils of the school) or they may choose to set up early years provision for the benefit of people who live or work in the locality using their community powers (in which case the children would not be pupils of the school). Legislation no longer requires the board to consult the local authority, school staff, parents etc., but a school should do this as a matter of course. In addition, schools are no longer required to have regard to guidance issued by the Secretary of State or the local authority when setting up community services.

15. Academy trusts may choose to run extended services and provide childcare, as well as run nurseries and children's centres. This may require a change to their Articles of Association. Academy trusts are advised to contact the EFA who will advise.

11.4.1 The 'charitable purpose' requirement

16. The board of a maintained school has the power to provide, or enter into contracts to provide any facilities or services that will further any 'charitable purpose' for the benefit of pupils at its school, families of pupils or people who live and work in the local community[86]. This power is in addition to boards' powers and responsibilities on the control and community use of school premises.

17. 'Charitable purposes'[87] may cover such services and activities as:

- childcare (including before and after school and during the holidays);
- adult and family learning;
- health and social services; and
- parenting support and other facilities of benefit to the local community. Examples include access to information and communication technology (ICT), or sports facilities.

18. This is not an exhaustive list and a wide range of services will be covered within the definition of charitable purposes. Any profits that a school may make from providing such services must be reinvested in the service or in the school.

[86] Section 27 of the Education Act 2002.

[87] The Charities Act 2011.

19. Since all academy trusts are charities, their charitable object (or objects) is (are) set out in its Articles of Association, together with the powers that the academy trust can exercise in pursuit of its charitable object(s).

11.4.2 Restrictions on extended activities

20. A board cannot engage in any activity that might interfere with its duty to promote high standards of educational achievement at the school. The board's use of the power is also subject to any limits or restrictions contained in the school's instrument of government or in its trust deed (if it has one) and to any local directions issued by the local authority regarding the control of school premises.

21. Before carrying out any plans to provide facilities or services using the power in section 27 of the Education Act 2002, the board must consult with the local authority, school staff, and parents of its school's registered pupils. The board can also consult some or all of the registered pupils, where the board considers this appropriate in view of their age and understanding and where the exercise of the power would affect those pupils, and anyone else that the board consider appropriate.

11.4.3 Ofsted registration and inspection for childcare facilities

22. Boards should be aware that schools do not have to register childcare provision for children over two separately with Ofsted, where:

- at least one of the children is a registered pupil at the school;
- it is provided as part of the school's activities; and
- delivered directly by an employee of the school.

23. Where a school engages childcare providers who are not required to be registered by Ofsted, it is advised to work only with providers who are registered on the voluntary part of the Ofsted Childcare Register.

11.5 School companies

24. Boards of maintained schools may form companies to undertake certain specified activities[88]. They can be formed independently or in conjunction with other boards and/or 'prescribed' third parties. This allows schools to purchase goods and services collectively, to provide services or facilities to other schools, or to carry out functions that a local authority is able to contract out.

25. The existence of a company allows individual boards to enter into contracts as a group and to pool resources without being part of a formal structural collaboration such as a federation. Schools are able to follow a well-established procedure for forming a company[89] and have considerable flexibility in how the company is run.

---

[88] Sections 11 – 13 of the Education Act 2002.

[89] The School Companies Regulations 2002; The School Companies (Private Finance Initiative Companies) Regulations 2002; The School Companies (Amendment) Regulations 2003 and The School Companies (Amendment) Regulations 2014

26. Where a company is formed, the board remains responsible for the running of the school: a school and a company are separate legal entities. It follows that if the company gets into financial trouble, there will be no risk to the school's assets or the employment of the school's staff. Teachers will not be expected to transfer to the company.

27. Boards of maintained schools must have the consent of their local authority to form or join a company. This can be refused only on certain specified grounds relating to the school's performance or financial management. Each company will have a supervising authority (a local authority) to make sure that the company is run on a sound financial footing.

28. School companies can make a profit. The articles of the company must state whether profits may be distributed to its members in line with the procedures set out in the articles and/or to further the aims of the company.

29. An academy trust's Articles of Association set out its 'object' and the powers that it may exercise to further that object. These powers include the power to establish or support any charitable companies or trusts formed for the trust's object and to set up subsidiary companies to carry on any trade or business to raise funds for the trust.

11.6 Parent councils

30. A Parent Council is a body of parents that represents parents and allows them to put forward their views to the headteacher and the board of their children's school. A Parent Council can be less formal and require a lesser commitment than being a member of the board. It allows more parents to contribute to their child's school. Boards of a 'majority governance Trust school'[90] must establish a Parent Council[91].

31. To meet the local needs of the school, the board of a 'majority governance Trust school' must decide which pupils (or groups of pupils) will require special consideration and whose parents are represented on its Parent Council. The board must also decide how parents are appointed or elected to the Parent Council and the term for which they should serve as members.

32. The Parent Council, in consultation with the board, agrees how it will operate. Whilst many Parent Councils manage themselves, the board should provide the information, support and assistance it reasonably needs to perform.

33. The board must consult the Parent Council about its conduct and carrying out its powers under section 38 of the Education and Inspections Act 2006. The board decides how, when and on which issues to consult the Parent Council, and is a matter for the individual school. The board must take into account any advice or views expressed to it by the Parent Council when it is conducting the school or exercising its powers[92].

34. Other maintained schools are free to choose whether to establish a Parent Council and determine its membership. This includes foundation schools in which the foundation or Trust appoints a minority of foundation governors.

---

[90] Where the Trust or Foundation appoints the majority of governors on the board.

[91] Section 23A of the Education Act 2002 (as inserted by section 34 of the Education and Inspections Act 2006).

[92] Section 38 of the Education and Inspections Act 2006 .

Section 12 – School finance

1. This section explains the financial responsibilities of governors. Section 12.2 provides information about financial requirements for academies. Sections 12.3 – 12.4 provide information about the financial accountability arrangements for maintained schools. Sections 12.5 onwards cover topics that apply to both maintained schools and academies.

12.1 Efficiency and value for money

2. In schools, 'value for money' means achieving the best education for children in relation to budget spent on the school. There is a wide range of tools available to support boards achieve value for money from a school's resources.

NCTL workshops for governors

3. NCTL has licensed the delivery of training workshops for governors on understanding and driving up financial efficiency in schools.

Benchmarking

4. The department provides schools' spending data annually in the performance tables. The data is grouped into categories of income and expenditure alongside measures of attainment. This allows schools, parents and the wider public to compare how schools spend their money with the outcomes they achieve. The Schools Financial Benchmarking website enables maintained schools to compare their spending in detail with other maintained schools, consider their comparative performance and think about how to improve their efficiency. Academies can view comparable statistical data for Income and expenditure in academies in England.

Procurement

5. As well as complying with basic procurement rules, all schools should ensure they are getting the best deal when buying goods and services. Schools can then reinvest these savings in their priorities for teaching and learning. GOV.UK has detailed advice on buying goods and services.

School business managers

6. Skilled school business managers (SBMs) have a big impact on the effective financial management of a school. They save headteachers' and teachers' time and help to ensure that resources are deployed effectively. The National Association of School Business Management has a range of information and resources available.

Collaboration

7. Schools working together have greater opportunities to generate efficiencies as they can pool funding, purchase services jointly and share staff, functions, facilities and technology across sites. Collaboration can also help schools raise standards and maintain local provision. The efficiency and value for money in schools section of GOV.UK provides more information.

12.2 Financial requirements for academies

8. Academy trustees have wide responsibilities to ensure their trust assets and funds are used only in accordance with the law, articles of association, funding agreement and the Academies Financial Handbook. Trustees have wide discretion over their use of funds, and are responsible for the proper stewardship of those funds by exercising reasonably discretion by ensuring value for money, regularity and propriety on all transactions and in all decision-making. EFA and independent auditors will look at academies to gain assurance over the regularity and propriety of spending. The Accountability system statement explains the system of accountability for schools in detail.

9. It is a requirement of all academy trusts' funding agreements to follow the Academies Financial Handbook, which sets out expectations on governance and financial oversight, alongside a structure of delegated authorities. Trustees should understand the Academies Financial Handbook in detail, and be aware of the Charity Commission's guidance The essential trustee: what you need to know, what you need to do (CC3) and Internal financial controls for charities (CC8).

10. Academy trusts have a number of other characteristics, which distinguish their financial management arrangements from those of local authority maintained schools, meaning that they:

   - must appoint a senior executive (usually the principal in a single academy trust and the chief executive in a multi-academy trust) as accounting officer (AO) who will carry an overriding and personal responsibility for the proper stewardship of public funds, including the securing of value for money, regularity and propriety;

   - must appoint a chief financial officer to act as the trust's finance director, business manager or equivalent;

   - are responsible, through their board of trustees and AO, for all financial transactions within delegated authority limits set out in the Academies Financial Handbook;

   - must establish a control framework and establish processes to provide assurance over the suitability of, and compliance with, its financial systems and internal controls; this includes the establishment of an audit committee or a committee which fulfils the functions of an audit committee, depending on trust income level;

   - must, because academies are publicly funded bodies and part of central government, participate in annual accounts consolidation exercises;

   - must approve a balanced budget each financial year;

   - must refer potentially novel and contentious transactions to EFA for explicit prior authorisation;

   - must maintain a register of interests, publishing as a minimum on their websites, the relevant business and pecuniary interests of members, trustees and local governors;

   - must appoint a registered statutory auditor and prepare annual financial statements in line with EFA's Academies Accounts Direction. The AO must also complete and sign a statement on regularity, propriety and compliance each year as part of the audited financial statements;

- can be subject to a published Financial Notice to Improve where weaknesses in governance or financial management are identified.

12.2.1 Liabilities

11. The academy trust must ensure that it has adequate insurance cover in compliance with its legal obligations or has opted into the academies risk protection arrangements (RPA). Not all risks are covered in the RPA (e.g. motor vehicles).

12.3 The accountability system for maintained schools

12.3.1 Accountability of boards through local authorities

12. Local authorities have to account for expenditure by maintained schools. They must publish these accounts and have them audited by external bodies. For this reason, each local authority has to put in place a system of financial controls that apply to maintained schools in its locality. Governors of foundation schools, voluntary-aided (VA) and voluntary-controlled (VC) schools are also charity trustees and must comply with charity law, in addition to any requirements placed upon them by their local authority. They may also have to work with a separate foundation that holds the land and buildings on trust for educational or religious purposes.

13. Local authority systems of accountability for schools are based on the principles of regularity, propriety and value for money. Guidance on Managing Public Money is available. Each local authority has an officer appointed by law (the 'section 151' officer) to make sure that its financial affairs are properly managed. This includes making sure that schools act within the agreed local financial framework, and that the authority has proper oversight of the funds it distributes to schools. Local authorities must report on their use of education grants to the department.

14. The Accountability system statement explains the system of accountability for schools in detail.

12.3.2 The school budget

15. Maintained schools receive a delegated budget from their local authority. More detail about the way this is calculated is provided in Section 12.4. Local authorities are required to maintain a scheme for financing schools that sets out the framework for the financial relationship between them and the schools they maintain[93] (the Scheme). The Scheme must include procedures for maintaining effective financial management, securing value for money and providing financial information to the local authority. The local authority must consult the board and headteacher of every school maintained by the local authority on any proposal to revise the Scheme, before submitting a copy of its proposal to the Schools Forum for approval[94]. Section 12.8 provides more information about the Schools Forum. The Scheme

---

[93] Section 48(1) of the School Standards and Framework Act 1998.

[94] Schedule 14 to the School Standards and Framework Act 1998.

must cover specific matters set out in regulations[95]. The current version of the Scheme must be published on a website. Statutory guidance on schemes for financing schools is available.

16. Under the Scheme, a local authority's responsibilities are:

   • reviewing schools' budget plans;

   • carrying out high level monitoring of school budgets;

   • agreeing a deficit reduction programme with schools in deficit;

   • challenging excess surplus balances held by schools without good reason;

   • planning and carrying out an audit programme for schools, taking into account their Schools Financial Value Standard (SFVS) returns (Section 12.3.4); and

   • intervening in schools causing financial concern.

17. These arrangements enable the board to spend the delegated budget, within the parameters of the Scheme and other statutory requirements. Boards can spend the budget delegated under the Scheme:

   • for the 'purposes of the school'[96] (usually taken to mean for the 'educational benefit of the school's pupils');

   • for the benefit of pupils in other schools[97]; and

   • to provide community facilities or services[98].

18. Schools can raise extra funds for example, by inviting donations from parents, businesses and others, by renting out premises, and undertaking other income generating activities. Boards must not use their budget share to subsidise the costs of activities that are not covered by the list of permitted activities.

12.3.3 Local authority requirements that ensure schools spend money in accordance with Schemes

19. Boards must comply with the requirements set by their local authorities. Although these will vary in detail, they are likely to require boards to:

   • cooperate with the audit regime set by the local authority;

   • use financial controls which meet local authority requirements;

   • seek to achieve value for money, for example by following local authority tendering requirements;

   • hold the school senior leadership team to account for expenditure;

   • submit an annual budget plan and provide monitoring data;

   • complete a Consistent Financial Reporting return annually;

   • keep an up-to-date register of register for all governors;

---

[95] The School and Early Years Finance (England) Regulations 2012.

[96] Section 50(3)(a) of the School Standards and Framework Act 1998.

[97] School Budget Shares (Prescribed Purposes) Regulations 2002 made under section 50(3)(b).

[98] Section 27 of the Education Act 2002.

- maintain a fixed asset register; and
- comply with local authority rules for unusual payments such as write-offs and severance payments.

20. In order to meet these requirements boards need to:
- assure themselves that the school keeps accurate accounting records;
- manage the school budget and agree expenditure in a way that meets local authority requirements for financing schools within the financial year;
- decide how far to delegate to the headteacher their powers to spend the delegated budget. They should set the financial limits of this delegated authority;
- determine the staff complement and a pay policy for the school (in line with STPCD);
- make sure no governor, employee or related party has benefited personally from the delegated budget, other than under agreed arrangements such as a contract of employment;
- make sure the schools' assets are under their control and measures are in place to prevent losses or misuse.

21. The board, or a committee of the board, must approve the budget each year and is accountable for managing the finances of the school. Boards generally scrutinise the budget through a finance committee. This allows governors to retain oversight of the decision-making process and to ensure the headteacher accounts regularly for the schools' spending. The board must assure itself that the school is securing value for money and acting with financial probity. The department strongly recommends that schools recruit one or more governors with sufficient financial skills and experience to undertake effective financial scrutiny.

12.3.4 Local authority responsibilities including the SFVS

22. Local authorities have a statutory responsibility to ensure that they secure good value for money in the use of their resources[99]. This includes resources retained centrally for the provision of services to schools as well as expenditure by schools. The requirement to secure good value for money is also a condition of their receiving the Dedicated Schools Grant (DSG). This is the main source of local authority funding for schools and is explained further in Section 12.4.

23. All maintained schools must complete the Schools Financial Value Standard (SFVS) each year. The purpose of SFVS is to help schools manage their finances, to support them in securing value for money across all of their spending, and to give assurance that secure financial management arrangements are in place. Governors, the headteacher and senior staff should consider the SFVS annually. The standard does not say what evidence the board should consider but governors must be confident that their response has a firm grounding. The school must send a copy of the signed standard to their local authority's finance department. All local authority maintained schools must complete the SFVS by the end of March each year and submit to their local authority for review.

---

[99] The Local Government Act 1999

24. Boards must demonstrate compliance through the submission of the SFVS assessment form signed by the chair. The form must include a summary of remedial actions with a clear timetable, ensuring that each action has a specified deadline and an agreed owner. Governors must monitor the progress of these actions to ensure that all actions are cleared within specified deadlines.

25. Local authorities and other auditors will have access to the SFVS returns. When they conduct an audit, they may check whether a board's self-assessment is in line with their own judgement. Auditors should make the board and the local authority aware of any major discrepancies in schools' judgements. More information on School and college funding and finance is available on GOV.UK.

12.3.5 Loss of the right to a delegated budget

26. The local authority may suspend a school's right to a delegated budget[100] in certain circumstances. These are where a board:

    ● has persistently or substantially breached a requirement or restriction relating to its delegated budget;

    ● has not managed its budget share satisfactorily; or

    ● has not managed in a satisfactory manner any expenditure, or sums received, in the exercise of its power to provide community facilities and services.

27. The local authority must serve a notice to the chair specifying the grounds for suspension and give the board and headteacher a copy of the notice. A local authority may also intervene to suspend a school's right to a delegated budget where there are concerns about standards[101]. The local authority is required to review the suspension within a specified period.

28. The principal effects on a school of suspension are:

    ● loss of the right to decide how the delegated budget should be spent; and

    ● loss of powers in relation to staffing matters.

29. Schools and local authorities ought to discuss problems that might lead to suspension and try to solve any problems before the need for formal action arises. Schools should co-operate with local authority monitoring of financial issues and take a proactive approach to their resolution.

30. Where there are concerns about financial management and/or governance in an academy trust, the Education Funding Agency has the power to issue a Financial Notice to Improve (FNtI). If an academy trust is subject to an FNtI, all of their delegated authorities and other freedoms are revoked.

---

[100] Schedule 15 to the School Standards and Framework Act 1998.

[101] Sections 59–66 of the Education and Inspections Act 2006.

12.4 The school budget

31. The funding system for maintained schools is based on the dedicated schools grant (DSG) and pupil premium. Most funding is provided through the DSG, which is currently allocated to local authorities based on historic data. Local authorities are required to pass on most of the money directly to schools and are only allowed to retain funding centrally under certain circumstances. Most of the DSG is distributed to maintained schools using locally determined formulae. To date, there has been significant variation in how local authorities allocate funding to schools. In order to move to a more consistent, comparable and transparent system, local authorities are now required to use much simpler formulae. They will be limited to a maximum of 12 factors in their formulae, which relate largely to pupil characteristics and pupil numbers (taken from School Census data), and less so on the circumstances of the school. Funding is available for pupils with high needs in special schools or mainstream school, based on the needs of the pupil.

32. The pupil premium is a separate funding stream to be used solely for the educational benefit of children eligible and registered for free school meals at any time during the last six years, or those who have been in continuous public care for six months. From April 2014, looked after children will attract funding from the first day of care, and eligibility will include those adopted from care or leaving care under a special guardianship order or residency order. The amount of funding will rise to £1320 for primary pupils, £935 for secondary pupils, and £1900 per looked after child. The purpose of the pupil premium is to narrow attainment gaps between those children and their peers. Governors should ensure that pupil premium funding is being spent on improving attainment for eligible pupils. Schools must publish online[102]:

    - the amount of the school's allocation from the pupil premium grant for the current academic year;
    - how it is intended that the allocation will be spent;
    - how the previous academic year's allocation was spent; and
    - the impact this expenditure has had on the educational attainment of pupils who were allocated the pupil premium.

33. Service premium payments of £300 are also made for children whose parents recently left the armed forces or who died in service, to address the emotional and social well-being of these pupils.

34. The year 7 literacy and numeracy catch-up premium is additional funding which enables schools to provide literacy and numeracy catch-up support for year 7 pupils. It enables those pupils that did not achieve level 4 in reading and/or mathematics at key stage 2 to be given the opportunity to catch up as quickly as possible. As for the pupil premium, the board should ensure that year 7 catch-up premium funding is being spent on improving attainment for eligible pupils. More information and advice is available on GOV.UK.

---

[102] The School Information (England) Regulations 2008 as amended by the School Information (England) (Amendment) Regulations 2012

35. The PE and sport premium is designed to help primary schools improve the quality of the PE and sport activities they offer their pupils. The Ofsted inspection criteria specifically states that, in making their judgement on the effectiveness of leadership and management in schools, inspectors will consider 'how effectively leaders use the primary PE and sport premium and measure its impact on outcomes for pupils, and how effectively governors hold them to account for this'. Schools are required to publish on their websites the amount of PE and sport premium received; a full breakdown of how it has been spent (or will be spent); what impact the school has seen on pupils' PE and sport participation and attainment and how the improvements will be sustainable in the future. Schools should also consider how their use of the premium is giving pupils the opportunity to develop a healthy, active lifestyle.

12.5 Charging for school activities

36. Boards and local authorities cannot charge for admission to a state funded school or for the provision of education, subject to the limited exceptions referred to in the Charging for school activities advice and supporting legislation[103]. Schools may also invite voluntary contributions for some activities, if they make clear that the contributions are voluntary and that the child's participation in the activity is not dependent on whether or not the parent contributes. No charge can be made unless the board or local authority has drawn up a charging and remissions policy, which must be made available to parents on request.

37. Academies are required through their funding agreement to comply with the law on charging for school activities.

12.5.1 School minibuses

38. Schools may only charge for transport in their minibuses if they hold a permit issued under section 19 of the Transport Act 1985. In some cases, the permit exempts the school from Public Service Vehicle (PSV) operator and driver licensing requirements. A permit is not required if no charge is made in cash or kind. Schools should apply to their local authority for a permit for each minibus they operate individually.

39. Any charges made may be used to recover some or all of the costs of running the vehicle, including loss of value. The school may not make a profit, even if it is intended to go towards the school's other running costs or charitable purposes. Further information is available from local authorities or the regional Traffic Commissioners. Statutory guidance on 'Home to school travel and transport' is available on GOV.UK.

12.6 Payments to governors

40. School governance in England is rooted firmly in the principle of voluntary service. The government is committed to maintaining and promoting this principle for governors of both academies and maintained schools. This is in line with charity law and corporate governance practice in other parts of the public sector.

---

[103] Sections 449–462 of the Education Act 1996.

41. There are limited, specific, circumstances in which individuals serving as governors can receive payments from their school. However, this should only take place where it is clearly in the best interests of the school or academy.

12.6.1 Governor allowances and expenses

42. The law[104] allows boards in maintained schools with a delegated budget to choose whether to pay allowances or expenses to governors and associate members of the board to cover any costs, such as travel or childcare, which they have incurred because of serving as a governor. Where they choose to do so, it must be in accordance with a policy or scheme. Payments can only be paid for expenditure necessarily incurred to enable the person to perform any duty as a governor. This does not include payments to cover loss of earnings for attending meetings. Travel expenses must not exceed the HM Revenue and Customs (HMRC) approved mileage rates, which are changed annually and are on HMRC website. Other expenses should be paid on provision of a receipt (at a rate set out in the scheme) and be limited to the amount shown on the receipt.

43. Where a board does not have a delegated budget, the local authority may pay allowances expenses at a rate determined by them.

44. Boards in academies are free to determine their own policy on the payment of allowances and expenses.

12.6.2 Payment for serving as a governor

45. Paying governors for their role as a governor is subject to very specific legal restrictions. This is true in both maintained schools and academies as set out below.

Maintained schools

46. There is no legal power for schools, local authorities or the government to pay members of maintained school boards for their duties as governors.

47. Schools that are performing very poorly may be 'eligible for intervention'. In these schools, the Secretary of State or the local authority with the consent of the Secretary of State has the power to replace a board with an Interim Executive Board (IEB). They have the power to pay members of an IEB they impose, if they chose to do so. Payment to IEB members should only be offered when this is in the best interests of the school.

48. The legal power also exists for the Secretary of State or the local authority to appoint any additional governors to a maintained school board if the school is 'eligible for intervention'. The Secretary of State has the power to pay any governors they appoint. However, they have not used this power to date, preferring instead to seek an academy solution for the under-performing school.

---

[104] The School Governance (Roles, Procedures and Allowances) (England) Regulations 2013.

Academies

49. Academy trusts are independent charities. Their governors are therefore also charity trustees who must comply with Charity Law. This means that they can only receive payment for carrying out trustee duties if this payment is specifically allowed by the academy's governing document or has express authorisation from the Charity Commission. For academies, this power is not currently in the model Articles of Association and any change to allow payment to trustees would need Charity Commission authorisation.

50. The Charity Commission will only authorise payment to academy trustees where it has been clearly shown to be in the charity's interests. They will consider issues like the reasons for payment, whether conflicts of interests are managed appropriately, whether the Principal Regulator (for academies this is the Secretary of State for Education) is agreeable and whether payment of any trustees is in the longer-term interests of the charity.

MATs

51. Like standalone academy trusts, MATs are charities. As discussed in Section 4, MATs may appoint local governing bodies or other committees to oversee individual schools or group of schools. The people who sit on LGBs or other committees are not charity trustees unless they also sit on the MAT board. That means that the charity law restrictions on payment to trustees do not apply to them.

52. However, the government expects voluntary service to remain normal practice for local governing bodies and other committees. The legality of paying people that sit on them does not remove academy trusts' duty under charity law to act only in the interests of their charitable objectives. Any multi-academy trust considering paying people to sit on their local governing bodies or committees should review very carefully, whether this is in the best interest of the trust and whether this would be an appropriate use of public funds. Our expectation is that any payment would most likely be for a time limited period, for example in relation to bringing in highly skilled individuals to oversee the turnaround of an underperforming academy. MATs must also ensure that they manage any conflicts of interest in accordance with their trust's Articles of Association.

12.6.3 Payment for services

53. In both maintained schools and academies it is legal for boards to pay for goods and/ or services, including those provided by an individual who is also serving as a governor, although the individual must not put themselves in a position where their personal interests conflict with their duty unless they are authorised to do so. If a conflict does exist, the board should first assure themselves that this is in its best interests and will better help it achieve its purposes. The board must manage, and be seen to manage, any conflicts of interest that may arise, and be open and accountable to those with an interest; there would be no advantage of using the services provided by the individual if the need to manage the conflict of interest outweighed the benefit.

54. The department places very clear expectations on academy trust boards in how they should manage any conflicts of interest. It is essential that all contracts and arrangements for payments of goods and/or services follow proper procurement processes. In addition, where a contract is awarded to an academy member, trustee or a party connected to them the service/goods must be provided at cost and no profit is allowed to be made. Full details of the requirements placed on academies can be found in the 'Academies Financial Handbook'.

55. Further information about payments to trustees is available in the Charity Commission guide (CC11), Trustee expenses and payments.

12.7 Responsibilities of charity trustees

56. Academies, sixth-form colleges, voluntary and foundation schools are 'exempt charities'. Unlike most other charities, schools that are charities do not have to register with the Charity Commission because they are exempt. As the principal regulator, the department monitors charitable schools to make sure that they comply with charity law. Governors of charitable schools must make sure that they:

- comply with requirements in the governing document;
- act responsibly and in the interests of the charity and its beneficiaries (who will be specified in the governing document);
- manage any conflicts of interest; and
- exercise reasonable care and skill, taking professional advice where necessary.

57. The Charity Commission document 'Charities and charity trustees – an introduction for school governors' provides further information. The Charity Commission website contains further information for charitable trustees. Information on the 'regulation of exempt charities' is also available on GOV.UK.

12.8 Schools forums

58. Each local authority must establish a schools forum[105]. It advises the local authority on the operation of the local Schools Budget. The forum has limited powers to make decisions about central expenditure by the local authority from the schools budget.

59. The schools forum[106] consists of members elected by the headteachers and school governors of maintained schools, academies and pupil referral units. In addition, there are other non-schools members to represent other relevant interests such as private, voluntary and independent early education providers and the local 14-19 partnership. Local authorities must also consider whether diocesan authorities should be represented. Whilst the balance between headteachers and governors on the forum is for local decision, both governors and headteachers of maintained schools can expect to be involved in electing members to the forum.

---

[105] Section 47A of the School Standards and Framework Act 1998.

[106] The Schools Forums (England) Regulations 2012 set out the required membership for Forums.

12.9 School premises

12.9.1 Ownership of land and buildings

60. Boards should know who owns the land and buildings from which their school operates. School land is usually owned freehold by the local authority, but leasehold interests are possible and there may be several parcels of land with different ownership arrangements that together constitute the school site. This is especially true of church land.

61. Boards who are considering academy conversion should refer to the detailed departmental guidance on GOV.UK. As part of this process, they should be aware of the need to consider transfer of land and buildings, in particular the need to engage trustees where appropriate.

62. In the majority of schools set up through private finance initiatives (PFI), the construction of the buildings are funded by a private sector contractor and their funders. The buildings are then operated and maintained by that private sector contractor for an agreed period, typically 25 years. The PFI contract will set out the maintenance programme. These contracts will remain in force even if the LA transfers its interest in the school land to the board, if the school converts to academy status. At the end of the contract term, responsibility for the buildings will revert to the board.

12.9.2 Disposal and protection of publicly funded school land

63. Under Schedule 1 of the Academies Act 2010, the prior consent of the Secretary of State for Education is required to dispose of any land – whether or not it is playing field land. Guidance on where consent is needed for any disposal (which will include granting leases) is set out in the Academy property transactions: advice and forms. Special protection is given to playing field land as set out in the Playing fields and school land: selling or change of use advice.

64. VA, VC and foundation schools have particular protection for their school playing field land. Under Schedule 1 of the Academies Act 2010, the prior consent of the Secretary of State for Education is required to dispose of any land – whether or not it is playing field land. Guidance on School land and property: protection, transfer and disposal is on GOV.UK. Further information is available in Playing fields and school land: selling or change of use.

12.9.3 Closure of a foundation or voluntary school

65. The board, foundation body or trustees must[107] apply to the Secretary of State when a foundation or voluntary school is to be closed. The Secretary of State will consider making a legal decision ('direction') about what should happen to that land, which was bought or improved at public expense.

---

[107] Part 2 of Schedule 22 to the School Standards and Framework Act 1998.

■SCHOLASTIC

12.10 Funding for capital investment

12.10.1 School Condition Allocations

66. School Condition Allocations are provided to local authorities and schools to support them in maintaining the condition of the school estate. Funding is allocated on a purely formulaic basis for LAs, including community and VC schools, VA schools, non-maintained special schools and sixth-form colleges. The formula uses pupil number data taken from the Annual School Census, and adds an element related to building condition in the area. Departmental advice on School condition allocations and devolved formula capital (DFC) allocations for 2015 to 2018 is available.

67. For academies, allocations for condition needs are made using either the Condition Improvement Fund (CIF), or direct formulaic allocations to multi-academy trusts (MATS). MATs will get an allocation in 2016-17 if (a) they have 5 or more open academies in the MAT on 1st November 2015 and (b) these open academies (or their predecessor maintained schools) had 3000 or more pupils, as recorded on the January 2015 census.

68. The CIF budget is administered by EFA and accessed through a bidding process.

69. Maintenance funding for VA schools is made available via the 'Locally Co-ordinated Voluntary-aided Programme' (LCVAP). The local authority, in discussion with the voluntary sector, agrees which projects from their maintenance allocation should be prioritised for funding. EFA administers LCVAP payments.

12.10.2 Basic Need Capital

70. 'Basic need' supports the capital requirement for providing additional pupil places both in new or expanded maintained schools, and academies. Basic need funding is allocated on a purely formulaic basis using data from the Annual Schools Capacity Survey. It is made available to local authorities in the first instance and it is for each local authority to decide how basic need allocations should be prioritised at local level. The local authority officer can supply further information on the planned use of basic need funding with responsibility for pupil place planning.

12.10.3 Devolved Formula Capital

71. Devolved Formula Capital (DFC) is capital funding that is allocated, via local authorities, on a purely formulaic basis and is made available to schools for their own use, in line with departmental guidance. DFC is based on the Annual Schools Census data set, collected in January. Local authorities should pass on the level of DFC, as calculated for each school by the department, to their schools and the EFA for academies. DFC is normally used for smaller capital purchases, including information and communication technology.

72. DFC is calculated for all maintained mainstream primary and secondary schools, special schools, pupil referral units, academies, community technical colleges and non-maintained special schools. Independent schools and nursery (direct grant) schools do not receive DFC.

73. Details of the school capital funding allocations: 2015 to 2018 available to local authorities and schools are on GOV.UK. The arrangements for VA schools are explained in the Blue Book guidance on capital funding for VA schools in England.

74. Information on capital funding, including advice on academies and VA schools, is available from: enquiries.EFACAPITAL@education.gsi.gov.uk

12.10.4 Developments at schools

75. The Building Regulations 2010 set standards for the design and construction of buildings in England and Wales. Their prime purpose is to ensure the safety and health of people in or around buildings, but they also cover energy conservation and accessibility. They cover the construction of new schools and many alterations of, and improvements to, existing school buildings. As with other building types, developments at schools are bound by normal planning controls. Information on these building regulations and associated guidance are on the government Planning Portal.

12.10.5 Arrangements for funding premises-related work at VA schools

76. Responsibility for capital work to VA school premises is shared between the board and the local authority. The standard rate of grant support to VA school boards from us is 90 per cent. Local authorities are able to help boards with their 10 per cent contributions, subject to their own spending priorities and budget availability.

77. There are special arrangements for the proceeds of sale of school land in voluntary schools, which can be found at School land and property: protection, transfer and disposal on GOV.UK.

12.10.6 School premises regulations

78. Regulations set minimum standards for the premises of all existing and new schools in England[108]. The regulations cover toilet and washing facilities, medical accommodation, health, safety and welfare, acoustics, lighting, water supplies and outdoor space. Departmental advice on standards for school premises is available on GOV.UK.

---

[108] As set out in the School Premises (England) Regulations 2012 and Part 5 to Schedule 1 of The Education (Independent School Standards) Regulations 2014. The latter covers academies.

Section 13 – Information sharing

1. This section details the roles and responsibilities of boards, headteachers, local authorities and other educational establishments in giving information to each other, parents, pupils and the Secretary of State for Education.

2. Any reference to parents in this section includes all adults with parental responsibility. It also acknowledges the rights, duties, powers, responsibilities and authority that parents have by law.

13.1 Information from the board to the Secretary of State

13.1.1 Information from academy trusts to the EFA

3. Academy trusts must provide EFA, or its agents, with the information required in order to exercise its responsibilities, and to meet funding requirements. This information must be of sufficient quality to meet the purposes for which it has been requested. The trust must provide the information when and how EFA and its agents request it. EFA will consider the impact on academy trust business in the deadlines it specifies for the provision of information.

4. On occasion, EFA will require urgent information from the trust, usually as a result of requests to EFA to fulfil its duties to provide information to the Secretary of State and account to Parliament. EFA will act reasonably in its requests for information and will have regard to the costs and timescales of providing the information, and where appropriate to its confidentiality. In requesting information, EFA will also consider information previously supplied by the trust to EFA or other stakeholders with whom EFA is realistically able to share information. EFA may also request information that the trust gathers to meet its own needs.

5. In the event that the trust does not return the information EFA requires by the specified deadline, or that the information is not of an acceptable quality, EFA may carry out whatever investigations it deems necessary to collect the information, where appropriate in consultation with the trust. EFA may deduct, as necessary, all or part of the cost of the investigations from EFA's recurrent funding of the trust.

6. The trust must notify EFA of:
   - the vacating or filling of the positions of chair of trustee, accounting officer and chief financial officer, including direct contact details; and
   - the appointment of all members and trustees within 14 days of that change.

7. Notification must be made through EFA's Information Exchange.

13.1.2 Edubase

8. Edubase is the department's register of educational establishments in England and Wales. It contains vital information about academies, maintained schools and Further and Higher Education colleges, used by the department and many key partners to update systems, contact schools, perform analysis and inform policy decisions, some of which might carry funding implications.

9. Edubase is the approved process for schools to inform the Secretary of State of their intention to join or leave a federation.

10. For those reasons, it is essential that all schools ensure their details are up to date on the Edubase website. For further information on how schools can login and update their details please refer to the EduBase FAQs.

13.1.3 Secure Access

11. The Secure Access Portal allows registered users access to the department's systems. Access to systems is granted on a user-by-user basis and only those systems that a user has permission to access will be displayed.

12. The board must reassure itself that mandatory data collections and statistical returns requested by the Secretary of State are given to the relevant timescales and security standards.

13. The board of an academy must also refer to its funding agreement and Articles of Association for details of information to be given to the Secretary of State.

13.1.4 Performance Tables and RAISEonline

14. Information from the school performance tables and RAISEonline provide a valuable tool to help governors monitor and compare school performance. The board must reassure itself that its school takes part in performance tables data checking exercises, run during September each year, to either confirm data accuracy or provide changes when required. The department informs headteachers in advance of when each checking exercise will start and when the checking website will become available.

15. Further information on RAISEonline and school performance tables is available in Section 2.

13.2 Information given to the board by the local authority

16. When a maintained school governor is appointed, they should receive background information from the local authority[109]. This should include a copy of the instrument of government for the school, which sets out the composition of the board.

---

[109] Regulation 31 of the School Governance (Constitution) Regulations 2012

17. The local authority gives the board and the headteacher financial information concerning the school.

13.3 Information from the board to the local authority

18. The board of a maintained school must give the local authority any relevant information or reports in connection with the discharge of the board's functions that the local authority may need.

19. Boards of all schools, including community and foundation special schools and academies must on request, provide certain information[110] to parents of pupils or prospective pupils, to local authorities and to primary care trusts, including:

    ● basic information about the school's SEN provision;

    ● information about the school's policies for the assessment and provision for all pupils with SEN; and

    ● information about school staffing policies and relationships with external partners.

20. Further information is available in the 'SEN Code of Practice'.

21. The board must publish the information in a single document and make copies available free of charge to parents, the local authority and the primary care trust. The local authority may publish the information referred to above if the board agrees. Where there is an agreement, the board must supply the local authority with the information, which must be published without alteration.

13.4 Information from the headteacher to the board

22. The headteacher must give the board any information asked for to help it carry out its functions.

23. An academy headteacher has a contractual relationship with the board. As the employer, the board would expect requests for information to be met.

13.5 Annual report to parents

24. Before the end of the summer term of each school year, headteachers of maintained schools are responsible for preparing and providing parents of all children in the reception year and above with a written report on their child's achievements. The information to be included in the annual report to parents is set out in legislation[111].

---

[110] Education (Special Educational Needs) (Information) (England) Regulations 1999.

[111] Schedule 1 of the Education (Pupil Information) (England) Regulations 2005 (and the 2008 amendments to the Regulations).

13.6 Information from the board to parents

13.6.1 School prospectus and publishing school information online

25. Boards of maintained schools are required to publish on a website the information specified in the School Information Regulations[112]. These regulations were amended[113] to remove the requirement for maintained schools to publish an annual prospectus. Schools keep the freedom to choose whether they wish to continue marketing themselves through a prospectus and/or publish on a website additional information they feel is necessary to meet the needs of parents and the wider community. Further information on what maintained schools must publish online is available on GOV.UK.

26. Maintained schools boards will need to reassure themselves that the school continues to meet any legislative requirements in developing specific policies and communicating them to parents. The department publishes advice on statutory policies for schools.

27. Academies must comply, by their funding agreements, with the relevant sections of independent schools standards prescribed under section 157 of the Education Act 2002.

28. The current model funding agreement requires academies to publish the same information on their website as maintained schools. Any academy should refer to its funding agreement for specific requirements.

29. All boards should publish on their school website up-to-date details of their governance arrangements in a readily accessible form[114]. Further detail of the information that should be published is available in the statutory guidance Constitution of governing bodies of maintained schools and in the Academies Financial Handbook.

13.6.2 Publishing School Performance Information

30. Schools must publish whole-school results from key stages 1–3[115]. The department also publishes national analyses of the results.

31. The headteacher must send the Early Years Foundation Stage Profile (EYFSP) results to the local authority. The board must send teacher assessment results for key stage 1 to the local authority (or, in the case of academies, the local authority or another accredited provider). The department also expects the results of the phonics screening check to be sent to the LA. Key stages 2 and 3 results must be sent to the STA. The local authority collects the EYFSP, phonics screening check and key stage 1 results and sends them on to the department.

---

[112] The School Information (England) Regulations 2008.

[113] The School Information (England) (Amendment) Regulations 2012.

[114] Readily accessible means that the information should be on a webpage without the need to download or open a separate document.

[115] The School Information (England) Regulations 2008 as amended by the School Information (England) (Amendment) Regulations 2012.

13.6.3 The Home-School Agreement

32. All boards of maintained schools and academies should reassure themselves that a written home-school agreement is in place[116]. Schools should consider the statutory guidance when drafting their agreements.

13.7 Pupils' information

33. The board of a maintained school should reassure itself that its school[117]:

   - keeps pupils' curricular and educational records;
   - provides access to these records to parents;
   - reports at least annually on their pupils' progress and educational achievements;
   - provides a report to school leavers; and
   - makes sure that the pupils' educational records and common transfer file (CTF) is transferred securely. [118]

34. The statutory duties described in the Pupil Information Regulations, such as those to provide parents with access to their child's educational records, do not apply to mainstream academies.

35. The Data Protection Act 1998 gives all pupils, regardless of age, the right of access to their own educational records held at school or by the local authority. In certain circumstances, a parent, on behalf of their child, may make requests for this information. The DPA's subject access rights only give parents the right to see personal information about their child when the child is unable to act on their own behalf, or gives their consent.

36. An academy's funding agreement itself does not place any statutory requirements on academy trusts about providing information to parents for individual pupils. Academy trusts must meet the Education (Independent School Standards) Regulations 2014 (SI 2014/3283). Paragraph 32(1) (f) in Part 6 of Schedule 1 requires them to issue an annual written report of a pupil's progress and attainment in the main subject areas.

37. The provision in the Pupil Information Regulations for the secure transfer of educational records applies to all schools throughout the United Kingdom. This includes transfers from maintained schools to academies and independent schools. However, the Pupil Information Regulations and the need to transfer educational records and CTF do not apply where a child changes schools between academies or from an academy to a maintained school.

13.8 Retention of pupil educational records

38. All schools are directly responsible under the DPA for the collation, retention, storage and security of all information they produce and hold. This includes educational records, headteacher's reports and any other personal information of individuals – pupils, staff

---

[116] Sections 110 and 111 of the School Standards and Framework Act 1998.

[117] The Education (Pupil Information) (England) Regulations 2005.

[118] For example, by using the department's Secure Access system as pupils change schools.

and parents. As such, many schools should consult their legal advisers and develop a data retention policy in accordance with the DPA.

13.9 Data Protection Act (DPA) 1998

39. Schools have direct responsibility for ensuring that they comply with the DPA and handle personal data in line with it.

40. The DPA places certain statutory obligations on schools. These include:

    ● notifying the Information Commissioner's Office (ICO) of the school's register entry (name and address of the data controller and a general description of how personal information is processed);

    ● providing a statement or 'privacy notice' to individuals, such as pupils and parents, whose personal data is being processed or held; and

    ● responding to requests for personal data or 'subject access requests' within 40 calendar days.

41. Schools should also consider:

    ● obtaining their own data protection and/or legal advice;

    ● formulating their own data protection or data handling policies;

    ● ensuring that staff understand and follow policy when handling personal data.

42. The department has published advice on Cloud software services and the Data Protection Act.

43. Data protection advice for schools is on the ICO website.

13.10 Freedom of Information Act 2000

44. The board is responsible for making sure that the school complies with the Freedom of Information Act 2000 (FOIA). It should also reassure itself that the school has in place a Freedom of Information publication scheme. The legal presumption of openness makes it more important that a school decides its policies and conducts its day-to-day operations in a way that stands up to public scrutiny.

45. As requests for information can be directed to the school through anyone who works there, the board should make certain that all members of staff are aware of the FOIA and how requests for information are handled by the school. Boards may choose to charge a fee, which must be calculated according to the Freedom of Information and Data Protection (Appropriate Limits and Fees) Regulations 2004. The ICO publishes guidance on its website.

46. Schools are under a duty to provide advice and assistance to anyone requesting information and must respond to the enquiry promptly, and in any event, within 20 working days of receipt (not including school holidays[119]).

---

[119] The Freedom of Information (Time for Compliance with Request) Regulations 2004, 2009 and 2010 exclude days that are not school days from the 20 working day period.

■SCHOLASTIC

Section 14 – Support to be effective

1. There is a wide range of services and resources available to help boards deliver their functions effectively.

2. The department publishes a termly 'Need to Know' package containing everything schools need to help them plan and implement changes during the academic year.

3. Following a decision by the contractor the Governorline service is no longer in operation. Pending the outcome of the Spending Review, a decision shall be made on offering the provision of the service out to tender. The department apologises for the disruption and suggests, for specific support, governors contact the alternative support listed within Section 14.4.

14.1 Recruitment

4. As discussed further in Section 3, the effectiveness of the board is fundamentally linked to the quality of the people involved. In 2015-16, the Department is funding 3 strands of free support to help boards recruit skilled people:

   - Academy Ambassadors, hosted by the New Schools Network, recruit senior business leaders to serve on the boards of multi-academy trusts

   - SGOSS Governors for Schools, recruits governors with specific transferable business and management skills to fill boards' skills gaps.

   - Inspiring the Future enables schools and colleges to search and identify online people from the world of work who are willing to offer support in a variety of ways, including as a governor.

5. The Inspiring Governors Alliance is the result of discussions between the department, NGA, NCOGS, CBI, SGOSS Governors for Schools and the Education and Employers Taskforce about how to work together to celebrate those involved in governance and increase both demand for and the supply of high calibre governors with relevant skills and experience.

14.2 Support from the NCTL

6. The NCTL is responsible for helping schools and their partners develop and deliver high quality continuous professional development and leadership training, as well as enabling successful boards to take on a lead role in school-to-school support to improve the performance of other schools.

7. The NCTL has developed a Chairs of Governors' Leadership Development Programme for vice, aspiring and existing chairs and is delivering it through 11 licensed providers. Further details are available on the NCTL website, including information about scholarships available to support participants to access the programme.

8. The NCTL organises expert peer-mentoring support to chairs of governors through the National Leaders of Governance programme, as well as providing a wide range of good practice information and resources for governors on its website.

9. The NCTL has also developed a new Clerks to Boards Training Programme and free training workshops for governors on three key policy priorities – understanding RAISEonline, performance related pay and financial efficiency.

14.3 Other training resources

10. Other resources and opportunities for induction training and continuous development include:

*   The NGA has developed Welcome to Governance, an induction resource for new governors and trustees. It covers both local authority maintained schools and academies;

*   The NGA published their eight aspects of effective governance for all boards and which feed into the All Party Parliamentary Group on Governance and Leadership's Twenty Key Questions for a school governing board to ask itself;

*   The NGA Chair of Governors' 360 Appraisal service provides an analysis of the chair's current performance, and aims to offer information regarding areas of strength, as well as areas where improvement may be required (there is a charge for this service);

*   The NGA has also published the APPG's Twenty-one Questions for Multi-academy Trusts – Key questions a MAT board should ask itself;

*   The New Schools Network's academy resource hub provides advice and resources on expansion as well as jobs, suppliers and events;

*   Guidance on the crucial role of the chair, developed jointly with the National Governors' Association (NGA), is available on the NCTL website. The NGA have also developed the Chair's Handbook, a guide for chairs and aspiring chairs (there is a charge for this publication);

*   Modern Governor is a leading provider of online training for school governors. They offer a number of e-learning modules, including one on 'Governor Induction and Skills';

*   Governor E-Learning (GEL) offer a Governor Induction Pack; a selection of generic tools which can be tailored to suit an individual board's requirements;

*   The NGA has developed a skills audit and matrix for boards, structured around the core functions of the board to help them identify skills and knowledge they need to deliver their functions effectively;

*   The NGA and the Wellcome Trust have jointly developed a Framework for Governance which provides guidance on how governors can evaluate their own practice, set the strategic direction for their school and monitor progress against this;

*   The NGA Model Code of Conduct helps boards draft their own code of conduct, one which sets out the purpose of the board and describes the appropriate relationship between individual governors, the whole board and the leadership team of the school; and

*   The National Co-ordinators of Governor Services' (NCOGs) resource Succession Breeds Success: How to Grow Leaders in your Board offers guidance on how boards can ensure continuity of leadership.

14.4 Other Support

11. Support for boards is also available from:

- Education Endowment Foundation (EEF) – an independent grant-making charity dedicated to breaking the link between family income and educational achievement;
- Freedom and Autonomy for Schools – National Association (FASNA) – represents the interests of self-governing schools to government, the National Employers' Organisation for School Teachers (NEOST), unions and other groups;
- Governor E-Learning (GEL) – an organisation developed by the Eastern Leadership Centre (ELC) in partnership with local authority governor service managers and governance consultants;
- Information for School and College Governors (ISCG) – A free advice service for clerks and governors
- Modern Governor – a subscription service developed by the Learning Pool providing online training and e-learning;
- National Governors' Association (NGA) – a membership organisation for school governors and trustees in England from both maintained schools and academies;
- The Key for School Governors – a membership service that provides guidance on school governance;
- Local authorities who provide guidance through their own governor support services;
- Other commercial governor support organisations; and
- Peer-to-peer support online – there are growing opportunities to share experiences with other governors online through groups such as UKGovChat which aim to enable governors to share good practice, and support and challenge each other.

Notes

FREE GOVERNOR RECRUITMENT SERVICE

We are SGOSS - Governors for Schools

We recruit
Volunteers

from
Businesses

for
Schools

over
8,000
since
Jan 2014

over
16 years' experience
working with
2000+ companies

"Your organisation have done more than anyone else in assisting us to not only fill a vacancy, but do so according to our needs."

Olwen Greenwood
Lakeside School

And we do it all for FREE

www.governorsforschools.org.uk
T: 020 7354 9805

■SCHOLASTIC

Build
a Reading School with
Book Clubs and Book Fairs

We're here to help you inspire readers. Kids who read succeed and your Book Club or Book Fair can improve a child's life chances forever.

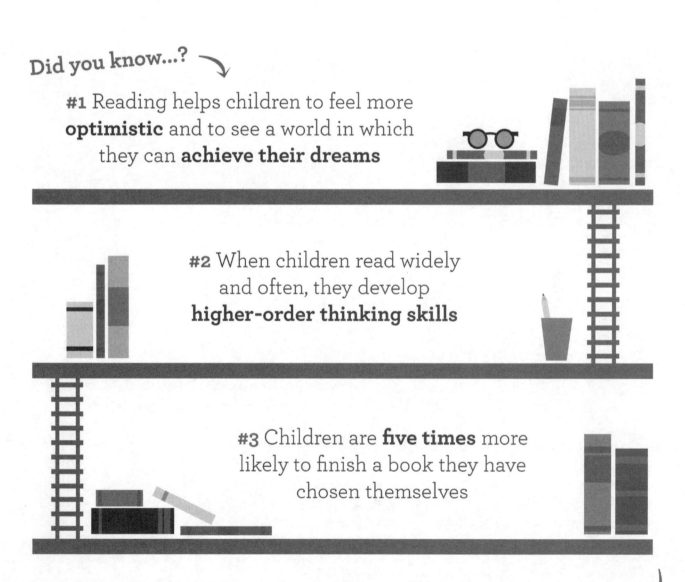

Did you know...?

#1 Reading helps children to feel more **optimistic** and to see a world in which they can **achieve their dreams**

#2 When children read widely and often, they develop **higher-order thinking skills**

#3 Children are **five times** more likely to finish a book they have chosen themselves

Find out how Scholastic Book Clubs and Book Fairs can help to build a **love of reading** in your pupils and earn **free books** for your school at
scholastic.co.uk/readingschool

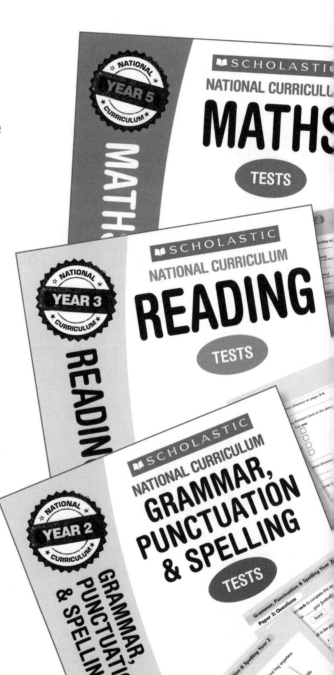